Stock Exchange Securities, an Essay On the General Causes of Fluctuations in Their Price

Robert Giffen

CK EXCHANGE SECURITIES.

STOCK EXCHANGE SECURITIES:

An Essay

ON THE GENERAL CAUSES OF FLUCTUATIONS

IN THEIR PRICE.

BY

ROBERT GIFFEN.

LONDON:

GEORGE BELL AND SONS, YORK STREET,

COVENT GARDEN.

1877.

ADVERTISEMENT.

THE origin of the following notes and observations is a very simple one. For eight years, between 1868 and 1876, the writer was connected as editor and contributor with important financial journals, and in that capacity came much in contact with the opinions of those concerned, whether as speculators, investors, or dealers, on the causes of change in the price of securities, principally securities of the Stock Exchange. He could not but be struck with the continual reference to general causes of change which those most familiar with the facts were constantly making, while it was his duty to reflect on the matter, and supply the public daily and weekly with his own explanations of the phenomena.

This reflection has since been continued amidst other avocations, and the result is the present attempt to systematize a little the observations of years.

The nature of interest-bearing securities and the laws of the changes in their price, are subjects which seem likely to increase in importance, both practically and theoretically. The writer's object will be gained if he assists in any way those concerned with securities, in accounting for the phenomena of their changes of price, and if he attracts the attention of political economists to what he believes will be practically a new field of inquiry and discussion.

R. GIFFEN.

44 PEMBROKE ROAD, KENSINGTON ;
June, 1877.

CONTENTS.

CHAPTER I.

PAGE

CHAPTER II.

CHAPTER III.

CHAPTER IV.

CHAPTER V.

CHAPTER VI.

CHAPTER VII.

CHAPTER VIII.

CHAPTER IX.

CHAPTER X.

CHAPTER XI.

CHAPTER XII.

STOCK EXCHANGE SECURITIES.

CHAPTER I.

INTRODUCTORY.

THERE is a great deal in theoretical books of Political Economy on the general question of supply and demand as regulators of price, and what is meant by the tendency or alleged tendency of the one to equal the other. In the following pages I propose as much as possible to keep clear of this discussion, which tends to degenerate into a mere logomachy. There is no doubt that in most markets, and as regards most articles within very wide limits, an excess of demand over the supply at a given price will raise the price, and an excess of supply will lower it. As regards articles also which are capable of being produced in variable quantities, a high price will bring out an increase of supply, and a low price will check it. For some purposes it appears unnecessary to define the meaning of supply and demand more exactly ; and the questions regarding price, and supply and demand as connected with price, which seem most to require discussion, relate to the nature of the influences which govern the motives of individuals in supplying and demanding particular articles or groups of articles, and so make it possible to trace a certain order in the variations of the prices of such articles.

That there is such an order in regard to one large group of articles—what are known as securities of the Stock Exchange—it will be a principal object of this Essay to show. An attempt will also be made to give some account of what this order is, and to demonstrate the necessary relations between the prices of this group and the prices of other articles, including the hire of money.

It will be convenient to explain at the outset what is meant by securities of the Stock Exchange. The word 'security' is a very general one. In the language of the money market, it means the title of almost any kind of property which can be given as 'security' for a loan. A bill of exchange, a dock-warrant, the titles of land or houses, mortgage deeds, may all be made use of, and are made use of, as securities for money lent. But the securities quoted on the Stock Exchange have certain peculiarities which are not the property of everything which may be a security for money. Their characteristic seems to be the combination of interest-bearing power, either actual, probable, or only potential and contingent, with the division of the article dealt in into equal parts, so as to be capable of exact definition and of being submitted to the speculative manipulation of a great market. It is obvious that other securities possess one or more of these features. Lands and houses, mortgages, bills of exchange, shares in private partnerships, capital employed by individuals singly in business, have an interest-bearing power of the same nature as the shares of joint-stock companies, or the debts of states, which are dealt in on the Stock Exchange. There are also articles capable of easy definition but without interest-bearing power, such as gold, corn, cotton, copper, pig-iron of certain brands, coffee, and probably others, which are all susceptible of being manipulated in a great market where there are crowds of dealers of various descriptions. But

the combination of interest-bearing power with
the facility of being handled like gold or cotton
makes a Stock Exchange article a thing *sui
generis*, whose fluctuations in price will conform
to an order of their own which can be traced,
although in doing so it will of course be necessary
to bring out much that is common to them
with other articles.

These definitions appear also to involve by
implication what the nature of the inquiry must
be. In distinguishing a great group of articles,
and inquiring as to the laws of their price, what
we really inquire into is not merely the nominal
money price of the articles, but the relation of
their price to that of all others which are the
subject of exchange, as well as the money which
is the medium of the exchange. We must not
think in such matters exclusively of the money
price. What goes on at every exchange is that
people sell corn, cotton, or other articles for
money only in the first instance; the whole
object of the sale is to enable them to purchase
something else, and if purchases as a rule did
not balance sales, apart from money, the whole
machinery of business would come to a dead
stop. If actual cash passed for all the articles

sold in a country on a given day, it would not take many days for the whole cash of the country to be in the hands of a few sellers, so that the rest of the people would have no money to work with. The exchange for money, therefore, only covers a real exchange which is always going on between the articles which the money from time to time represents. What we may call the ultimate transactions in money, that is, transactions in which money in its narrowest sense is actually acquired and kept in the form of coin or bullion, are comparatively few, although such transactions are, no doubt, specially important in all questions of price.

The great groups of articles for which Stock Exchange articles are exchangeable may also be simply described. Particular securities must either be sold for other securities of the Stock Exchange; or in exchange for interest-bearing securities which are not quoted on the Stock Exchange; or in exchange for other articles, that is, for consumable commodities generally, using the latter word in its widest sense, so as to include such articles as diamonds and valuable pictures which seem little destructible, and also certain articles like corn, cotton, or gold, which are capable of being manipulated in a speculative market, but have not the property of bearing interest.

What are the laws of price then which affect the special article we have defined ?

CHAPTER II.

THE CONNEXION BETWEEN PRICES AND THE QUANTITY OF MONEY.

It is laid down by writers on political economy and currency, though the practical application of the rule must be attended with difficulties, that the quantity of money in a country regulates the aggregate price of all articles. A hundred thousand pounds of gold will theoretically serve for the exchanges of a country as well as a million or ten million pounds. The nominal prices will be different, but the smaller nominal sum in one case will be as effective as the larger nominal sum in the other. The rule is correct of course only within certain conditions. To give it validity, it must be assumed that a scarcity of money produces no expedients for economising money, and that an abundance of money does not lead to want of economy, which can hardly ever be the actual conditions of life. It must also be assumed that the quantity of commodities to be exchanged remains constantly the same, that the motive power of money is equal at all times, and that exchanges are effected at an unvarying rate of frequency, though in point of fact as we shall see the greatest changes in these respects are constantly taking place. But allowing all the conditions in which the rule applies to be fulfilled, we should still have to reckon as causes of change of prices generally the variations in the quantity of money in a country. An addition to the circulation raises all prices, a deduction from it lowers them. But this change is only nominal; the real prices are all the while unchanged. The same quantity of labour exchanges for the same quantity of corn that it did before, or the same quantity of corn exchanges for the same Stock Exchange security, and matters are equalised. As we have said, it is most difficult to show this rule, because the economies of money, the quantities of commodities, and credit, are daily changing things, but the theory in the abstract is a mere mathematical expression, and can hardly be disputed.

It follows then—the quantity of money in a country and its effectiveness and the quantity of commodities for exchange remaining unaltered —that if there is a general fall in money price in one group of articles, this means a rise in money price in all the other groups. And a general rise in one group means an average fall in all the others. If this were not so, a certain part of the money in the country would in the one case be thrown out of circulation, which is contrary to the hypothesis, or a certain quantity of money would be added, which is also opposed to the hypothesis.

And such changes of money price would on the hypothesis also correspond to real changes in the relation between two groups of articles. Say it is a fall in the money price of securities; this would mean that securities command a smaller quantity of other articles than they did before. On the other hand, a rise in the money price of securities would mean a greater command over other articles given to the holder of securities. The difference would also count both ways. In the first case supposed, that of a fall in securities, there must be, on the assumption made, a rise in the money price of other articles as well; in the second case there is not only a rise in securities, but a fall in the money price of other articles.

The real changes in the relations of the two groups of articles are not measured merely by the change in the money price of one, but by the sum of the opposite changes in the money price of the two.

Of course it is quite obvious that in the real world the hypothetical change in the relations of two groups of articles here described can hardly ever be traced. As already mentioned, neither does the quantity of articles to be exchanged, nor the amount of money in circulation, nor the state of credit on which depends the effectiveness of money, ever remain for two days the same. The rule, however, must be laid down as descriptive of a condition underlying the phenomena of the markets, and which will always be more or less operative.

Several corollaries from this principle are likely to be of practical importance. A change in any one of the conditions stated will have a great influence both on the aggregate price of securities and other articles which we may shortly term commodities, and on the relations of the two groups to each other. Thus an increase of the quantity of consumable commodities or of securities will have the same effect on the markets as a diminution of the quantity of money in circulation, unless there are simultaneous changes in the state of credit, or economies in the use of money, making the existing quantity more effective; such an increase of the goods offering for exchange must alter the money level of price. It is possible that the alteration will at first be confined almost exclusively to the group of articles which is increased. The whole fall in the average level of price will be due to a special fall in the group, which will alter its relation to the other groups very materially. But this does not follow necessarily, and it does not follow that permanently the change will be confined to the group in which the increase of quantity takes place. All that can be affirmed as mathematically certain on the hypothesis assumed is, that an increase of securities or commodities, like a diminution in the quantity of money, will cause a general fall of prices; and a diminution of articles, like an addition to the quantity of money, a general rise.

In the same way a variation in the frequency of exchanges at different times will have an effect on prices which need not be particularly explained. More frequent exchanges, unless other circumstances interfere, will require more money to maintain the former level of price, and less frequent exchanges will require less money.

It is another corollary of the principle that if there are natural limits to the quantities of commodities or securities which can be produced, and limits also to the changes in the amount and effectiveness of money, and the frequency or infrequency of exchanges, then there will also be natural limits to the rises or falls in prices which are possible. An indefinite general rise or an indefinite general fall will be an impossibility. As the natural limits on either side are approached, a movement of price which may have seemed uncontrollable will be checked. Whether there are such limits or not, and what they are, will be one of our inquiries. It will also follow from these principles, that any great change in the price of a particular kind of commodity or species of security implies a disturbance of relations among securities and commodities in general ; and this circumstance, according to the known qualities of human nature, will itself contribute to make it unlikely that the change will be of a permanent kind, unless there is some substantial change in the motives for the purchase or sale of the article. There must always be continual changes in the estimation in which particular articles are being held by mankind, but the presumption is against violent changes being enduring.

Another point of practical importance to attend to in consequence of the rule laid down will be, that in looking at a general rise or fall in prices, due to a change in the quantities of articles or money, or in the effectiveness of money, we must never overlook the nature of the real changes which this general rise or fall may conceal. Unless everything rises or falls *proportionately* in its money price, there will be an incessant real change in the relations of all articles to each other. If securities fall more than commodities, this will mean a general rise in commodities; and if commodities fall most, this will mean a real rise in securities. If most commodities and most securities fall, this may mean an important real rise in the exchangeable value of those which remain stationary. It is unnecessary, however, to follow out in detail the points to be thus attended to in consequence of the differences between real price and money price.

CHAPTER III.

THE CAUSES OF VALUE IN SECURITIES, IN RELATION TO COMMODITIES.

HAVING described in the previous chapter the abstract theory of the price of securities, and the meaning of a rise or fall, we have now to inquire as to the conditions under which the theory practically operates, and what are the main causes of a general rise or fall in price to be attended to.

We begin with the most general causes which can affect the value of securities. In a community where there is an economic equilibrium, where production and consumption balance each other, where the investment of fixed capital proceeds *pari passu* with the increase of population, and where the quantity of money in circulation increases only in proportion to the business done, it is quite clear that an adjustment of some sort will have been effected between the price of

securities and that of other commodities. Apart
from the changes due to the varying state of
credit and other transitory causes, a community
in such a state will insensibly have settled down
into the acceptance of certain notions which will
fix the relative desirability of certain articles and
their relations one to the other through the
mechanism of exchange. For our present purpose
this means that a certain average rate of interest
on capital will be accepted, and this will govern
the price of securities by which the yield on the
capital invested in them to the actual holders of
that capital is regulated. If the yield is judged
so low by holders of securities that the former
rate of saving is checked, or if it is judged so
high by the owners of consumable commodities, or
the labourers and capitalists who can create them,
that there is a constant bounty on the further
saving and investment of capital, so far there
will be no equilibrium, but conditions will exist
which will cause changes in the relative prices of
both securities and commodities.

It is, perhaps, hardly necessary to inquire
what are the causes which determine a community
at a given period to accept a certain average
yield on its capital. It is quite clear that in

this respect there is a constant play of opposite motives. A high average yield on capital is a bounty on saving, and a low yield will to a certain extent check saving. Whether it is true, as some hold, that there is in modern communities as actually constituted, a tendency of profits to a minimum which would be a tendency to an almost indefinite rise in the price of securities, it is, perhaps, almost unnecessary for the present to discuss. All we point out now is, that this quality of interest-bearing will be valued in a certain way in a community in equilibrium, and that this is what is meant by the price of the securities of that community.

We must notice, however, that this quality of interest-bearing is necessarily not the only cause of variation in price amongst securities themselves, and that the rate of yield is not everything, even as regards the relation of securities to other commodities. As all know, the prices of securities relatively to each other vary much, and they are likely, as human nature is constituted, to vary much. Some are in larger bulk, and for that or for other reasons are more marketable. The yield of some is better secured, or thought to be better secured, than others.

These are all causes for indefinite variations in the prices of individual securities. To a certain extent also the qualities of the securities which a community possesses will affect the rate of yield at which the price will be adjusted. If a community is itself unstable, and capital more or less insecure, the adjustment will probably be made at a higher rate of yield than if the community were stable and capital well protected. The bounty on saving and investment will require to be stronger in one case than in the other, and at a point it may cease to operate.

It is also noticeable that there will probably be a certain relation between the current rate of yield on fixed investments and the rate for money lent, principally the rate of discount on bills of exchange and the rates for short loans. In both cases the object aimed at is a certain yield for capital, and it makes no substantial difference that this is effected in the one case by the purchase of a title to property, and in the other by a loan which is to be repaid. In buying, an investor or capitalist provides or ought to provide a sinking fund against depreciation, in case he should have to sell at a capital loss; and in lending,

c

he also insures in various ways against a loss of capital; the provision for the sinking fund or insurance in both cases affecting the net yield. What the exact relation will be between the yield on fixed investments and that on floating capital or money lent will depend on many circumstances—on the amount of money which it may be the *custom* to keep floating, for instance —but a relation of some sort must exist, which will tend to be re-established if it is disturbed from any cause.

The nature of this relation can, however, only be perceived when long periods of time are taken into account. It must not be supposed that every sudden change in the hire of money in the short loan market will be accompanied by corresponding changes in the price of securities. There is a close connexion indeed between the short loan market and the speculation in securities. The funds of the short loan market are employed partly in holding securities, and where these funds are diminished or increased from any cause, however temporary, there is an immediate effect on the price of some securities. But the great mass of securities will only be affected by more permanent changes in the rates obtainable for money in other markets, and it is of this more permanent relation we have here been speaking.

Applying these rules to the most general causes of the disturbance of economic equilibrium in a community as far as securities are concerned, viz., the increase of consumable commodities on the one hand, and the increase of securities on the other, we have to affirm that an increase of consumable commodities, where the rate of yield on capital is not at the minimum, will lead to a real rise in the price of securities, i.e., to a fall in the yield. That such an increase will cause a money fall in all articles on the average (the amount of money and its effectiveness being unchanged), has already been noticed; but it would also seem certain that ordinarily it will cause the greatest fall in the kind of articles increased, i.e., consumable commodities. Unless there is simultaneously a total change in the estimation of securities as related to commodities, the increased offer of commodities will in fact mean that the owners are willing to exchange them for a smaller mass of securities than they did before. The result will also be a stimulus to the creation of securities. The desire for saving arises instantly the profit is made, and those who make the saving having either money or money's worth in their possession, seek an investment for it. The equilibrium is accordingly disturbed. The holders of fixed capital have no motive to part with it, for the necessity for reinvestment would be immediately felt. The money or money's worth, therefore, goes a-begging, the holders constantly offering to buy for a smaller and smaller yield, until in the end the yield is so small that they no longer offer, or some one pays labourers to make something which it is hoped will yield an interest to tempt them. The only limits to the rise in securities, besides the natural one of the command over commodities given to the holders becoming excessive, are the inclination of the holders of commodities to keep in kind or spend rather than invest, and the creation of new securities, which means in fact the absorption of a portion of the capital which is seeking investment.

In the actual world, should there be a change in the amount of money or its effectiveness at the same time that there is capital seeking investment, the apparent money rise in securities may be even greater than the real rise, or it may be less than the real rise, but the real change in

the relation between securities and other articles
will be what we describe.

The opposite contingency of an excessive
creation of securities, causing a fall in them in
relation to commodities, seems at first sight
impossible. You cannot make new investments
without actually using up new commodities.
Confusion may be caused by engagements to
invest beyond the savings of a community, but
the investments themselves cannot be made. To
a certain extent, however, it would seem that
they can be made. Unawares, a portion of the
means of a community required for consumption
may be diverted to fixed investments. To restore
the equilibrium, it becomes necessary to create
more consumable articles than formerly in a given
time ; and while this is being done a certain
portion of the invested capital gets to be on offer
for the purpose of obtaining articles of consumption. In other words, securities fall through the
excessive multiplication of them, and the dis-
proportion thus brought about between them and
consumable commodities. Should there be a
decrease of money or its effectiveness at the
same time, the fall in money price will be marked,
as well as the fall in the price of commodities ;

but the money fall will also conceal a real fall in securities in relation to commodities.

As regards Stock Exchange securities in particular, it must further be noticed that the increase or decrease of consumable commodities seeking investment which can affect their price, must be an increase or decrease in what is offered in the general markets. If people who have a surplus of such commodities use them in extending, say, their business premises, or in some other private manner, or finding a deficiency stop their current rate of outlay in fixed works, securities dealt in on the Stock Exchange cannot be affected. It is only therefore the general surpluses or deficiencies which are in question, and these, it is believed, are often much smaller than would be supposed beforehand. The most natural destination of savings is in their private conversion into fixed capital under the control of their owners. New houses are built, or old houses extended and enlarged; business premises are enlarged or improved, or better equipment provided; perhaps a new business of an analogous kind is set on foot; perhaps additional floating capital is employed in the business, so that it may be conducted with ease and facility. It is only in comparatively small quantities, if we think of it, that savings are available for the creation of new securities of the kind quoted on the Stock Exchange, or that such securities are sold on balance for the purpose of obtaining commodities to be consumed; were it otherwise, the real disturbance in the relations between securities and commodities would be incessant and tremendous. If a small amount of commodities offering in excess must cause a considerable rise in securities, and a small amount of securities on offer in excess a considerable fall, it is plainly most unlikely that the excesses are at any time very great. The changes great excesses would produce would immediately produce reaction.

As business is now conducted, also there would seem a further condition to the applicability of an excess of commodities, other than money in its narrowest sense, in raising the price of securities generally. This is, that transactions must take place in them, so that they can be represented by deposits in a bank, against which cheques can be drawn. So long as they are in the possession of the people who create them, or who have bought them without requiring to

borrow for the purpose, they are not in the form
of money, into which they must be converted
before they can be exchanged for securities in a
general market. But how are they to be converted into money ? To this the answer must be,
that the holders must either sell them to some
one for money, coin, or for a cheque upon a bank
by a purchaser, which that purchaser, *ex hypothesi*,
can only have the means of drawing by previously borrowing from a bank, or the owner
must himself pledge his excess of commodities
with a banker, so that he can buy securities with
the money so placed at his command. This is a
plain deduction from the nature of the business of
banks, the deposits in which must always be represented either by actual cash, or by re-deposits
in other banks, or by loans or investments. These
deposits can only be increased by an actual increase of cash, or by a loan upon credit, the
amount of which is directly or indirectly re-
deposited. Hence we affirm that an excess of
commodities likely to affect the general markets
for securities must become the subject of an
operation by which its value can be drawn
against ; some one, in fact, must borrow upon it,
so that the deposits in the banks may be in-

creased. We shall see afterwards in what various ways the deposits in the banks may vary according to the state of credit, and how all-important this is in the question of the price of securities ; but we only call attention to the one fact at present, that an excess of commodities offering for investment which appears to be, and which probably is, a very potent natural influence in raising the price of securities, can itself only become operative by an increase of cash in the hands of the public or at the banks, or by a credit operation at the banks. In other words, the condition of savings affecting the markets for investments is itself probably a change in the state of credit which permits an increase of borrowing, so as also to permit an increase in the quantity of commodities held.

In the same way a diminution of commodities likely to affect markets for securities must be such a diminution as produces a diminution of the deposits — the surplus money — in banks. A destruction by fire of commodities appropriated privately for consumption where the loss is wholly borne by the immediate sufferers would have no appreciable effect in lowering the price of securities. The commodities consumed were not an offer in the general markets, and the loss is gradually made good by the privation of the people affected. But if the destruction is of an article on which a bank had made advances, the deposits in the bank are, somehow or other, reduced by an equivalent sum. When the advance falls due, it is either not repaid and has to be written off, or it is repaid out of other funds which the borrower from the bank possessed, whose deposits are *pro tanto* reduced. The money offering in the general markets is accordingly less than it was, and the force to support prices at the former level is weakened.

CHAPTER IV.

THE EFFECTS OF CHANGES IN THE AMOUNT OF MONEY AND STATE OF CREDIT IN THE PRICE OF SECURITIES, AND THE NATURAL LIMITS OF SUCH EFFECTS.

WE have discussed in the last chapter the influence of an excess of commodities or securities on the price of the latter, on the assumption that the amount of money and state of credit remain the same. It will be evident from what we have said, however, that the questions of the amount of money and state of credit are themselves perhaps the most important elements in question. We believe that they are the most important, and the two are so inextricably intermixed that we discuss them together.

First, as to the amount of money. We need add nothing in general to what we have already said as to the effect of this factor. It is a mathematical deduction, that if the amount of articles

and the habits of dealing in them remain unchanged, a deduction from the quantity of money
will cause a fall in prices, and an addition to the
quantity of money a rise. This is, of course,
only a change in money prices ; and if all articles
are affected proportionately, there is no change
in real relations. But there is a peculiarity in
securities which causes them and other commodities to be affected disproportionately by what
seems a proportionate rise or fall. The property
of the securities with which we are dealing is to
yield an interest. At the same time, therefore,
that an increase in the quantity of money causes
a rise in prices, it tends to diminish the yield of
securities in two ways : more nominal capital
is required to procure the same nominal yield,
and this nominal yield is less effective as regards
commodities than it was before. A decrease of
money causing a fall in securities along with
other articles would, on the contrary, be accompanied by an increased nominal yield, which yield
would at the same time be necessarily more
effective measured by commodities. To a certain
extent, if a proper adjustment is to be made between
securities and commodities when the quantity of
money is increased or diminished, the effect of

the change in the real value of the security itself, by the change in its real yield, must be allowed for. In the actual world this change would alter the point at which there would be a bounty on saving, or a check to it.

A change in the state of credit, which is equivalent to an increase or decrease in the quantity of money, will have precisely similar effects. The real yield of securities is altered by each general rise or fall in the mass of articles, and this real alteration cannot but have an influence in checking the general movement. When securities rise along with a rise in commodities, the yield from them to the capitalist diminishes in two ways, and there is consequently a smaller bounty on saving, with a greater stimulus to create new securities. When securities fall along with commodities, the bounty on saving is increased by the greater nominal yield to be obtained, and the greater real value of the same nominal yield. In the latter case, there is at the same time a less temptation in one way to create new securities than when securities are high, because those who create them have to undertake a greater annual burden than at other times; although in another way the temptation may be increased, because the prices of all articles used in the fixed investment are lower.

But while these limitations exist to the effects of a change in the amount of money or state of credit, increasing or diminishing the effectiveness of money, there is a third limitation to the effects of a change in the state of credit in the natural limits of the possible degree of credit itself. On the one side there is usually a minimum amount of good credit, which exists even in the most depressed times. It is now inconceivable that the ordinary agencies of economising money—bank-notes and deposits with bankers, against which cheques are drawn, or such an institution as the clearing-house—could pass out of use, or have their effectiveness seriously diminished. What we are chiefly concerned with here is the change from time to time in borrowing power, and even here there is a large minimum of credit. Many firms and institutions are always able to borrow at a price, or what comes to the same thing, to make purchases on credit, and this potential credit is, I believe, so great that the phenomenon of an indefinite fall of prices is inconceivable. When this fall has gone the length of changing greatly the relation of prices to money in circulation, so that money goes farther than it usually does, the holders of money, and those whose credit remains, are able by their purchases to restore an equilibrium. In actual fact, the ordinary motives of human nature may be relied upon to induce them to purchase.

But on the other side there is also a maximum amount of good credit. No matter the solidity or reputation of firms or individuals applying for loans, the amount which banks or other intermediaries can lend is limited by the amount of real money at command. Say a banker has to keep half the amount of his liabilities in cash, the limit to the credit he can give is measured by this necessity. The moment his deposits are twice the amount of his cash, the amount of his lending must cease. In actual fact, then, the process of extending credit, which seems at first sight indefinite, because the loan which is made to A. is re-deposited directly or indirectly, and then re-lent to B., is not really indefinite. These re-deposits are constantly increasing the liability of the banker, and at a point he must draw the line. Whether it be a half, a third, a fourth, a tenth, or a twentieth of his liabilities, which he must keep in cash, does not matter. The limit exists, and every banker knows that as it is approached he must carefully consider what he is doing. Private individuals or firms giving credit to purchasers, are of course limited in the same way as bankers by the extent of their cash resources.

The limit is also likely to be the sooner felt in this way, that a general rise of prices, which is the effect of credit, tends to disperse cash. It must be accompanied by a rise in wages, and by a greater movement of all kinds in business, and this means the dispersal of cash into the hands of non-banking classes. More money goes into the hands of labourers and annuitants; there is more travelling even among the classes which keep bank accounts. Thus, the store of cash which is so serviceable as a basis of large credit operations, is apt to melt away as the effect of that credit.

We see, then, how much actual circumstances are likely to conspire against the continuance of extreme changes in general prices. A general rise of prices means the greatly diminished value of securities to the purchasers of them, and a premium on the creation of new securities; a general fall, the greatly increased real value of such securities, even if they have nominally fallen. A general rise also requires more money or credit, or both, to support it, but creates a state of things in which money disappears from the reserves of banks where it is required to support credit, and in which for this and other reasons the maximum of good credit is likely to be overstepped.   Apart, therefore, from the mechanism of markets, and the particular modes in which changes of prices are brought about, there is an inherent difficulty in extreme changes of general prices.   They imply a change in so much besides, if they are to be maintained, that we may be morally certain they will not be maintained.

There is little doubt, we may add, that of the causes of change we have been discussing the change in the state of credit is by far the most important.   The excess of commodities offering in the markets and available for raising the price of securities at one time as compared with another is likely to be inconsiderable.   The amount of money also in comparison with the great transactions of the market does not change much. There is no annual addition to its quantity which would not be easily used up by a comparatively small change in the state of credit with its accompaniment of a rise in wages, greater movement in business, and the dispersal of cash.   But credit

D

is an impalpable element, and may soon cause a change of millions upon millions in the amount of loans and advances. When credit improves, bankers keep lending on the best security, and redeposits keep coming in until it is found that the relations of money to loans and deposits are entirely changed from what they were. The causes of the changes in the state of credit would therefore seem to be the most important to be investigated for our present purpose.

Of these we notice first the diffused knowledge of the natural limits to credit, which helps to set in motion the inevitable reaction when any extreme is approached. Apart from all other causes, the knowledge that prices are 'above the average' will induce a change in the disposition to sell among holders, and a change in the disposition to buy among investors or speculators. Before, therefore, the natural limit which would in any event set bounds to a rise is reached, another real limit is overpassed with which it is in vain to struggle. No doubt sales by holders who must reinvest can only have a partial and temporary effect ; the disposition to keep money uninvested cannot be reckoned permanent, but occurring as it usually does, when the natural limits to credit rises are being approached, the anticipation has a great effect. In the opposite case of a great fall the anticipation of a reaction is almost equally effective.

In any case as regards changes in the state of credit, it must also be recognised that, like other great changes of opinion among mankind, they will take place in waves, and swell gradually to a maximum and decline gradually to a minimum, without any sufficient reason which can be stated. All that can be said is, that, according to a long experience, credit does change in this way. When it is at a low ebb we may be sure that the stream of tendency will once more be towards a return of the flood; when it is at the flood the tendency will again be to ebb. It is also to a certain extent intelligible, why the effects of changes in credit should tend to multiply themselves. Every reduction of credit causes a disturbance of relations between securities and commodities which produces a shock on the holders, and so leads to a further reduction of credit. In the same way any improvement of credit diffuses an agreeable feeling among holders of securities and commodities, and makes them feel richer, so that there is a greater disposition to lend as well as more money actually in hand for that purpose. If at the time when credit is changing, such real changes as the relative increase or decrease of commodities and money should co-operate, it is at once explicable how there should be great cycles of prices, and combinations of circumstances raising prices at one time and depressing them at another.

CHAPTER V.

THE INFLUENCE OF THE STOCK EXCHANGE.

WE are dealing with Stock Exchange securities, and we have now to inquire, What special influence is exerted by the organization of the Stock Exchange or the mode of doing business which has grown up there? Within what limit does that influence operate in modifying the application of the general laws, applicable to all securities, which have been described?

Stock Exchange is merely the name given to a private club, the members of which make it their business to buy and sell securities either on their own account or on commission. Abroad similar associations have been taken cognizance of by the governments which interfere with their internal arrangements; but in this country the club is free to act within the bounds of the ordinary laws. In any case, the circumstance of the club being controlled or not makes little difference for our present purpose. The main question we have to answer is, in what way the association of a number of people to deal in securities affects the price of the article dealt in.

It will be obvious, we think, that no such association can have any effect in altering the more general rules laid down. If prices **are** regulated at all by the quantity of money in a country, no association can prevent their being affected by the quantity of money. In the same way, if the existence of an association raises or depresses the money price of securities, it cannot prevent such consequences from the rise or depression as the change in the real return from the securities themselves in proportion to the capital represented by the market price. The association, if it has influence at all, must have influence within narrower limits.

The tendency of such an association, as with all similar associations, is probably to prevent some of the more extreme and occasional fluctuations. In no market are the sales or purchases by the public, as it is called, likely, at any given time or on any given day, to equalise each other. On the contrary, sales will be attempted on days when there are no purchasers, and purchases when there are no sellers. Hence, and for other reasons, the convenience of a set of dealers, who keep or borrow a stock of the articles dealt in, to which they add when sales are pressed, and which they diminish when purchases are in excess. The necessary influence of such a body is, as a rule, to prevent extreme fluctuations. Competition ensures that the seller will not be suffered to offer his commodities at too low a price, or the purchaser to buy at too high a price. The difference between the two prices is reduced as near as possible to the amount of profit which is necessary to tempt the intermediaries to operate.

Probably, also, the existence of such a body, disposing of a considerable capital and credit, tends to keep up the level of the prices of securities above what would otherwise be maintained. It is difficult to estimate what the effect of such a fund is, because it, or an equivalent fund, might have been used to keep up the prices of securities by means of permanent investment if it had not been employed in the business of the market. But it is easy to see that the withdrawal of the fund, or any large portion of it, at a given moment, would certainly have an effect in lowering the prices of all securities. It would disturb the ordinary adjustment which other causes had effected.

Nor can the methods of business followed on the Stock Exchange have any great influence in modifying these effects. The intermediate dealings on the Stock Exchange are carried on mainly by what are known as 'time-bargains.' All bargains of purchase or sale are arranged to be settled on certain fixed days, instead of for cash at the moment. But such an arrangement is essentially of the same nature as the credit given in any other business. A householder who arranges to settle his household bills fortnightly or monthly, exactly follows in the former case the practice of the Stock Exchange as regards the great bulk of its business; and in the latter case, the practice of the Stock Exchange as regards account dealings in home Government securities. Strange as it may sound, the householder who buys coals, or meat, or bread, to be paid for at the end of a fortnight, or at the end of a month, enters into that very mysterious time-bargain which is often, for reasons we shall explain presently, the opprobrium of the Stock Exchange. No doubt at the end of the fortnight or the month, there are facilities on the Stock Exchange for renewing the time-bargain, or extending the original credit; but such facilities are also common in all business, the peculiarity of the Stock Exchange being that the terms for which credit is given on each occasion are shorter, as a rule, than what is known in any other business. Essentially, therefore, Stock Exchange bargains are like all others, and can have no unusual effect in raising or depressing prices, apart from the fact that the short terms of credit may have ordinarily a restraining effect on speculative movements, and in some cases may precipitate a panic, on account of the magnitude of the mass of engagements coming due at once.

In actual fact, however, although there is nothing in the essential nature of Stock Exchange transactions to distinguish them from any other, the impression is well justified that the system conduces to what can only be described as pure gambling. In all speculative markets, where the articles are divisible into like and easily defined qualities, the same phenomenon is seen. The keen study of the causes of price affecting the article, and the application of capital to dealings in it, by limiting the current fluctuations of price, furnish the opportunities for bargains far beyond the means, or which threaten to be far beyond the means of those concerned, should anything unusual occur. People with 5000$l.$ (say), seeing the usual fluctuations in consols within a short period, to range between $\frac{1}{8}$, $\frac{1}{4}$, or, at the outside, about $\frac{1}{2}$ per cent, enter into engagements to buy consols for re-sale on the assumption that their risk is only about $\frac{1}{2}$ per cent. Consequently, as a $\frac{1}{2}$ per cent on 100,000$l.$ is only 500$l.$, they argue with themselves that if they are prepared for the risk, they may reasonably become practical intermediaries in the consol market to the extent of 100,000$l.$ In other words, the article being one of stable price, a little money goes farther in supporting price than the same money in a more fluctuating article. But this facility and temptation have gone the length of enabling many without even the 5000$l.$ to speculate in large amounts, and whose operations, because they can stand no loss, because every turn upwards or downwards is a fortune or ruin to them, mean sheer gambling, and the gambling of gamesters who are staking everything, and more than everything, they have. It is unfortunately to be feared that certain portions of society and the general business world participate in this gambling, and there is a good deal of other business conducted on the gambling principle, which it is impossible to eradicate. The gambling in no case is possible without credit, and where there is credit, while human nature remains as it is, there will always be undue credit. But the Stock Exchange gambling will not, any more than the legitimate Stock Exchange speculation, materially affect general prices. It tends necessarily, as a rule, to equalise prices, like the legitimate speculation it imitates, and it favours a panic when anything unexpected happens. It would seem, however, that as a counterpart to many evils, it may possibly sometimes mitigate a panic after the first stages, on account of the constant opposition there is between opposing sets of speculators, so that when anything unexpected happens there is a large class of people to profit by it, and so provide a market which would not otherwise exist, for all those who wish to buy or sell.

CHAPTER VI.

ON SYNDICATES, RIGS, AND CORNERS.

In the preceding chapter we have discussed the effect of the ordinary constitution of a Stock Exchange on the prices of securities. There is no power, as we have seen, in the natural operations of such a body or its members to take them out of the general laws affecting dealings in securities, but it is well known that on the Stock Exchange there are often combinations by which extraordinary effects on the price of particular securities, or groups of securities, are sometimes produced. It will be useful to inquire under what limitations these combinations act, and to what extent they can vary the operations of the natural laws we have described.

In making this inquiry, we must begin by one or two definitions. A 'syndicate' may be taken as a general *alias* for any combination of speculators on the Stock Exchange to force prices in one direction or the other. It is oftenest used in the narrower sense of a combination or partnership to introduce and sell a newly-created security to the public. The public have been made familiar with it in connexion with those disgraceful operations in so-called foreign loans, which were the subject of an inquiry before a Select Committee of the House of Commons in 1875. But the term is also used more generally in connexion with operations in all securities; and its use in regard to new securities is in reference to operations of substantially the same nature as those which take place in old. A syndicate is simply a clubbing together of certain persons to make particular purchases or sales in common. Say it is to buy in order to sell at a higher price: the manager of the syndicate makes the purchases and sales for himself and his partners, debiting them with the loss or crediting them with the profit, as the result of the operation may be, and, if necessary, calling on them to divide amongst themselves the balance of stock left unsold when the term for which the syndicate has been formed expires. What happens in regard to a new security different from what takes place in regard to an old security, is simply

that the syndicate make their purchases from
the promoters or creators of the new security,
instead of buying in the open market, as they
might do in the case of an old security. Many
syndicates have, however, been formed in old
securities where the purchases are chiefly made
wholesale from one or two large holders of the
securities, or where these large holders have combined to make a syndicate amongst themselves,
with power to purchase a certain quantity besides
of the floating stock in the market. In the contrary case, where a syndicate is formed to carry
out an operation for the fall, that is, to make
sales of stock for the purpose of re-purchasing it
at a lower price, the operation is usually in an
old security, or in a security of recent creation
which has so far passed out of the hands of the
original combination that it can be the subject
of hostile speculative combinations.

And the operations of such syndicates are
usually accompanied by market manœuvres which
are described generically by the name of 'rigs.'
The operation of purchase in order to re-sell begins
with an attempt to clear the market of all the
stock in the hands of dealers, whether the professional dealers of the Stock Exchange, or the

non-professional dealers, including outside speculators and members of the general public who
hang about the markets and are ready to turn
over the securities they hold at a profit. Having
possessed themselves of this stock at as low a
price as may be,—all kinds of manœuvres, such as
fictitious dealings in the Stock Exchange, false
reports about the value of the securities, mis-
leading articles in newspapers, which are got to
be inserted through corruption, fraud, or neg-
ligence, and the like, being resorted to for the
purpose,—the syndicate proceed to make bids for
stock which nobody has got to sell, and so the
price is raised. Their expectation is that a world
of minor speculators, seeing a steady rise in
price, will be induced to follow the lead, and
that investment money will be turned in the
same direction. The syndicate, also, hope that
these purchases will be so large as to enable
them to get rid of what they have themselves
purchased at an average profit. They will not
be able to sell all they purchase at the top price
of the market; they may even have to sell a
part at a less price than they paid, but on the
average they expect a higher price. If they have
been able, as they sometimes are, to commence

the operation by manœuvres to produce many speculative sales for the fall, that is, sales by speculators who have not the stock they sell, the chances of profit are so much increased; these speculators for the fall being, in fact, partially subjected to a cornering operation which we shall presently explain.

On the other hand, the operation of sale in order to re-purchase, when effected by a syndicate, is accompanied by manœuvres of a similar nature. The market is sustained by a semblance of purchases, by extravagant reports of the value of securities spread about the Stock Exchange, by puffs in the newspapers, or merely frequent mention, which almost answers the same purpose on the principle of forcing a card in conjuring, and by other arts which it would be useless to describe. Then when sales have been effected on a market thus sustained, which will naturally be most ripe for the operation just after a rise on which a previous syndicate has got quit of a great deal of stock, and left it in the hands of weak and uncombined speculators, the syndicate for the fall commences to offer stock on a market where there is already a disposition to sell, and where no one is inclined to buy. Offers upon offers are made, all kinds of false and true rumours to the prejudice of the stock are circulated, and so the game goes on. There is a 'rig' downwards, as in the opposite case there had been a 'rig' upwards. The peculiarity of both operations is that one set of speculators preys upon another, and that the public sometimes is very little concerned, although extreme movements are apt to attract the investing public to buy or sell just when they ought not to do so, and so play into the hands of speculators.

A 'corner,' again, is an incident in the working of rigs, arising from the constitution of all such speculative markets. It is a counter-rig to which a rig for the fall is liable. In a rig for the fall, sales are made by speculators who have not the stock they are selling. They engage, say on the next settling day, to deliver so many thousands, or millions, of five per cent 'Turks,' or North Western Railway stock, or some other security. If the stock is called for they must borrow it from some holder for a consideration; or, what comes to the same thing, pay the buyer a consideration to postpone taking delivery. Naturally, in a market where operations go on like these, there are many engagements to buy stock entered

E

into by people who are without the means of
paying, as well as engagements to deliver by
people who have not the stock, so that arrangements to postpone delivery are effected usually
with ease. Usually it is the buyer who has to
pay a consideration, which is then called in Stock
Exchange slang a 'contango;' but in many rigs for
the fall, the contrary is the case, and the sellers of
stock have to pay, their payment being called a
'backwardation.' It is a very common manœuvre
of the syndicates when they wish to buy or sell,
to pretend for a time, in the first case, that they are
not able to pay, and so raise the contango; and in
the second, that they are not able to deliver, and
so raise the backwardation, so as to induce the un-
wary to act in an opposite sense to themselves and
facilitate the whole operation. But when 'backwardations' increase from real causes, that is, a
great excess of speculative sales over speculative
purchases, the opportunity for the counter-rig, or
corner, begins. It is self-evident that if a stock
is not very big, and it cannot be increased, the
speculators for the fall can be placed at the mercy
of their opponents. As I have heard it explained,
if there are sales of 10,000 curl-papers of a peculiar description which cannot be newly fabricated,

and if there are only 9000 curl-papers of that kind actually in existence, the sellers of the 10,000 are liable to be 'cornered.' To be relieved from their engagement to deliver the 1000 curl-papers, which actually do not exist, they can be made to pay absolutely any price which those to whom they have made the engagement may fix. Few corners have been carried to this extreme point, for various reasons, but the theoretical danger of the speculator for the fall is manifest.

In what way, then, are such operations affected by the natural laws governing the price of securities, and what are the limits due to such laws or otherwise, of the movements in prices they can affect?

It is obvious, to begin with, that no syndicate or syndicates can have much permanent influence on prices or securities *generally*. They cannot buy up all securities and so raise the level, or go on offering securities and so depress the level, without disturbing the entire relation between miscellaneous commodities and securities. A rise in securities, as we have seen, means a fall in commodities, and *vice versâ*, and the disturbance would make itself felt beyond the power of combination to control. For this reason the operations of syndicates are confined to small groups of securities. Even in a considerable group they are, however, difficult. Any special buying in such a group must use up, *pro tanto*, the common money of the market, and cause other securities or commodities to exchange for less than they otherwise would do. In a very small group of securities the effect of this disturbance would not be noticed, owing to the vast resources and elasticity of the money market; but the limitation in principle exists, and constantly tends to prevent the more ambitious efforts into which riggers might be tempted.

And in the smallest groups of securities there are always natural limits to a rig or a corner. The condition of profit in either case is, that sufficient operations in a contrary sense to those of the syndicate should be induced; and it is most difficult to secure this condition, so that riggers, for their own interest, avoid extremes. Say the operation is to buy up some stock which has been long in existence. It is very easy, of course, for speculators who possess or can borrow sufficient money to buy up the whole of this stock, which, perhaps, can be done for a million of money or less. But this is not all they have to do. To make a profit they have to buy up at an average low price, and then they have to take the risk of other speculators and the public coming in to buy. Unless they can secure themselves by inducing sales for the fall at a low price, it is usually most doubtful whether they can induce purchases afterwards. There is also this difficulty in dealing with old securities. Such securities are held with varying degrees of firmness, but there is a great deal of the worst held which can never be bought at the very low prices, and some of which—sometimes a good deal—is sure to be sold at the high prices. For various reasons sales of securities are always taking place. Estates have to be wound up; people realise to go abroad, or for purposes of exchange, or to make good losses in business or speculation; consequently time is always working against a rig for the rise, and the only chance for the operators is that they can induce *unusual* purchases when they themselves wish to sell. In addition, when a great rise takes place, a strong interest to induce sales and prevent purchases is created. Brokers usually know what stocks their clients possess, and to those whom they have an opportunity of seeing they give advice to sell when there is a rise. Many holders are shrewd enough to act without such advice. The syndicate, therefore, which has forced a rise has to elect between taking a great deal of stock thus offered, trusting to its power of after-sale, or seeing the market slip away and its hope of profit disappear. On the other hand, if the operation is to force down a particular security, the whole force of the money-market is against the rigger, provided the security has solid value. Its interest-bearing capacity remains unchanged by what the rigger can do, and a fall beyond a certain point would induce many purchases by solid capitalists who know what they are doing, and are not to be imposed on by the rumours of the market. This and the fears of a corner are always likely to prevent speculators for the fall from carrying their operation to an extreme.

Where riggers appear most successful is when they anticipate a rise or fall of prices due to real causes; an operation for the fall in a particular security is likely to go far when the cycle has turned and almost all securities are discredited; but such appearances of success are not to be confounded with the effects which are really due to the 'rig' operations themselves and which are really very limited. Such 'rigs' cause great local dis turbances and individual losses, but they are fully controlled by the greater laws affecting securities.

How limited the effect is may perhaps best be shown by reference to one or two conspicuous illustrations, which need not be exclusively from the markets for securities. The 'gold' market in New York has, perhaps, furnished the most dramatic illustrations of a nearly perfect corner. Gold is like a security in its ease of definition and the interchangeability of parts; and in the United States where gold is a special money largely used in special operations of paying customs-duties, and interest on the Government debt, it has long been a commodity suitable for the manipulation of a great market. Speculators deal in it according to their estimates of whether it will be scarce or not. The result in American experience has been several remarkable 'corners,' which were promoted by the ease of bottling up the small quantity of gold about, the interval of time necessary to attract supplies, and the custom in the American market of daily settlings, which compelled the unhappy speculators who were cornered to pay backwardations daily. But these corners were always broken up whenever they came to a crisis. In the autumn of 1869 the price was actually forced up from 137½ to 160 in two or three days before the crisis came, and the Government interfered to beat the 'ring,' selling part of the stock of gold it had accumulated for paying its interest, and bringing back the price again in *half an hour* to 135 ; but even without this interference a few days would have seen the end of it. Gold was always coming from the mines, and there was practically an unlimited stock in Europe which could be attracted. In any case it is doubtful if the riggers in such cases ever make much profit, owing to the quantities they must buy in forcing up the market and the surpluses thus left on their hands.

On a smaller scale there have been rigs almost as remarkable, on the London Stock Exchange, of which I shall only mention two. One was in Anglo-American Telegraph stock in the spring of 1873. The origin of this was a counter rig or partial corner. Certain speculators knowing of the introduction of a new Atlantic Cable Company, the Direct, became 'bears,' or sellers for the fall of the stock of the Anglo-American Company, which had been previously established. The prospect of competition they calculated would weaken the dividend-earning power of the Anglo-American Company, and perhaps would cause discredit of all such property. But the time was in one respect unfavourable, as there was much money about, and all securities tended to be at a high level. A good deal of Anglo-American stock was also well held, being distributed through the country in small holdings; and what was held by speculators for re-sale was mostly in the hands of people interested in keeping up the price of all cable property. The speculators for the fall were consequently in a difficulty about borrowing stock to deliver, and the opportunity was seized by an opposing band of speculators. Purchases were made largely with borrowed money, and in this way the market scarcity increased. The price rose and rose, till from 133 at which it stood about the middle of January, it touched 176 in the early part of March, though the last price only held for a very short time. At the time nothing apparently could stop the rise, because some of the only holders of stock in large quantities were offering to buy, and no one would venture speculative sales. But each rise produced increased pressure on the part of brokers to induce clients to sell; there was perhaps treachery on the part of some large holders who had only partially combined. At any rate, sales of stock for delivery began and increased, and once the current changed the counter riggers were in daily increased danger. They could venture to take up no more stock, no others would buy, the constant sales rapidly depressed the price ; and as the operation had been supported with borrowed money, the fall of price was itself a cause of sales of stock, those who had made the advance being apprehensive of the security. By the middle of May the price was again under 140. The short time of the high price was a mere interlude in the great business of the market.

The other operation I have to refer to was on a still larger scale, and was not so much perhaps the work of a single syndicate. This was the 'rig' in Midland Railway ordinary stock in the autumn of 1874, its remarkable feature being the long continuance of the period during which speculators for the fall were compelled to pay backwardations. The beginning was the circulation of reports that the Midland dividend would be greatly reduced, and it was favoured by the circulation of similar reports respecting other railways. The result was that before the declaration of the Midland dividend in August 1874, the prices of the stock which had been nearly 140 at the beginning of the year had been forced down to 125, backwardations having been paid each fortnight for nearly three months previous. But speculators had miscalculated two ways. The reduction of dividend was very much less for that half-year than had been anticipated, and against this cause of fall in price was to be set a steady tendency of the public to set a higher value on such securities which had in fact been rising comparatively in value. The result was an 'explosion' of price upwards, the price quickly rising from 125 cum div. early in July, to 136 ex div. in September, and many incautious speculators being ruined. Here all the forcing of speculators for the fall had no appreciable effect, except for a short time, and the extreme fluctuations of price were after all as nothing to what often takes place in markets for commodities. The extremes are great for speculators on the Stock Exchange, because values there in all solid securities are brought to a high pitch of stability under the influence of competition, but in themselves after all they are of moderate extent.

In general, we conclude that the importance

often attached to these syndicates is greatly
exaggerated. At certain times, when securities
all tend to rise, the syndicates and speculators
have some power to concentrate the force of
the upward current on one or two groups of old
or newly-created securities. At other times,
when securities all tend to fall, they have a
certain power of inducing sales of special securities
and so precipitating their collapse. But their
power is exercised at great risks to themselves,
does not upset any general laws, and does not
interfere with the general levels of price, which
these laws tend to establish at different times.

CHAPTER VII.

ON FICTITIOUS SECURITIES.

WE have been describing the operations of syndicates on the Stock Exchange, as they may take place in any description of security, whether it is good or bad. There are frequently, however, dealings in a certain class of securities which are wholly sham articles, which possess intrinsically none of the qualities that are supposed to give them value, which are only sustained by mistaken opinions on the part of those who hold them, and by manœuvres of designing men, to which these opinions owe their origin. Although, strictly speaking, the dealings of syndicates with such securities are only extreme cases of attempts to force up prices of particular securities to an artificial level—and they can hardly be carried to great lengths for a long time, on account of the disturbance they must occasion according to the principles we have laid down—it yet seems ex-

pedient to consider separately the various effects
upon other securities of these dealings in fictitious
articles, and particularly the effects of the depreciation or total disappearance of such securities
from the markets when the cheat is discovered.
Along with the last case may also be considered
the rarer case of a considerable real change in the
interest-earning power of a security which may
sometimes amount to its total extinction.

There is obviously a certain facility for creat-
ing fictitious securities on the Stock Exchange at
certain times. During periods of high prices for
commodities, in addition to the real profits which
are made through the increased productiveness of
the industrial machine, and which are represented
by increased investments of fixed capital, or the
increase of the stocks of commodities, or the
increase of actual cash held by a community, there
is also an immense mass of what we call paper
profit, which is merely a swelling of nominal
values, whether of commodities in general or of
securities. Purchases of all articles and of securities are made by means of borrowed money ;
the sellers of such articles become consequently
the possessors of larger deposits at their bankers,
and these deposits in turn seek investment which

would inevitably have the effect of inflating prices still further. At such times the fictitious security makes its appearance, and with the aid of the sanguine feelings of the moment the creators of it find the market ready for their manipulation. The current which is carrying up the general level of prices is in fact diverted for a time into the channel of so-called new securities, the entire price of which in fact constitutes a part of the general inflation.

But it is equally obvious, as indeed arises from the mere statement of the nature of such fictitious securities, that, *pro tanto*, they must tend to depress the price of all other securities, or of commodities in general. The money in the country being only equal to a certain work, any additional demand upon it takes away a certain quantity from that work, causes the work to be done by a diminished quantity, and so lowers all prices. The effect is not traceable when the new demand is small, and sometimes even when it is large, owing to the great elasticity of credit; but we cannot doubt its powerful influence if the additional demands are at all on a considerable scale, and if credit for the moment is not proportionally elastic. Apparently what occurs at a time of inflated prices is that the fictitious security, being a form of additional infla-tion, becomes a source of further general inflation, so long as there is no shock to credit—adding to the instability of the money market equilibrium, arising from the smaller and smaller proportion of cash to the total nominal liabilities and banking deposits of the country. But as soon as a shock to credit comes, and general prices tend to dwindle, the competition of the fictitious securities is seriously felt. Other securities will probably fall more in consequence than they would do if there were no such securities. There can be no doubt, I think, if any one will consider the facts, that the presence on the markets of such bogus companies as the Emma Mining Company or the Lisbon Steam Tramways' Company, and many more, and to a far greater extent of such fictitious securities, or partially fictitious securities, as the loans of Honduras, Paraguay, Costa Rica, San Domingo, Peru, Spain, and Turkey, had for many years—one year with another—a steady influence in lowering the price of the more solid securities with which they competed. If mankind were suddenly to take a fancy to set a value on counters of any sort, such as the curl-papers already referred to, or the tulips in which the Dutch had a mania last century, or the china in which there is a mania at the present day, the effect would be precisely the same.

It usually happens, however, when there is a shock to credit, that the cheats in various securities, as in other articles, are discovered one after the other. Interest ceases on a loan on which there was high interest to be paid, but which interest was in fact never paid except out of the subscribers' money. A bogus company is found to have no earning power; instead of paying dividends to its shareholders, it goes into liquidation. Oftentimes the artificial level of price has only been maintained by most culpable loans on the security itself, or by the purchases of a highly speculative class whose other adventures come to grief, and who must consequently sell the fictitious security to meet losses. In these various ways the bladder comes to be pricked, and the fictitious security is exposed. What happens in any such event?

The first answer would be, of course, that if the fictitious security competes with others in the way described, its removal from the competition will tend to raise the price of the others. And so

F

it will permanently, and one year with another, we cannot doubt. But in actual fact, the immediate effects of the depreciation or disappearance of a particular security are probably very different. They occur at a time when every new exposure is a shock to credit. They consequently provoke further sales of all securities, further discredit, further running off of margins given by weak borrowers, and further exposures.

There is apt, in fact, to be a prolonged period of discredit, during which the apparent influence of the depreciation of sham securities is only damaging. It seems especially important that by any great fall in securities the dealers in them, including in that word not only the professional dealers on the Stock Exchange, but, as already explained, a vast mass of outsiders, are likely to be impoverished. It is they who hold largely the speculative articles, they suffer accordingly, and a certain fund for supporting the prices of almost all securities is accordingly diminished. The fund only passes perhaps into different hands, but in those hands it may be diverted to securities not quoted on the Stock Exchange, or to some other employment. In time, no doubt, when the special causes of discredit pass away, the more thorough the exposure has been the higher will be the recovery in the price of the more solid securities. There will be so much less of the sham article in competition with them. But this is an after, and not necessarily an immediate effect.

I think it has been observable, however, during the depression of the last few years, and the successive depreciation of one fictitious security after another, that the improvement in price of many of the higher descriptions of securities was not delayed, but simultaneous. This improvement has not been in all securities, but mainly in the highest class. But such an improvement does not alter the fact that time after time the successive shocks have depressed temporarily the prices of many securities not of a fictitious kind. Of this there was a conspicuous illustration, I believe in the spring of 1876, when there was a great fall in English Railway Stocks, owing to various causes, one of which will afterwards be noticed (see *postea*, p. 118), but another of which was, no doubt, the inability of the Stock Exchange *entourage*, impoverished by the fall of foreign securities in 1875, to maintain the purchases they had made. This fall in a few months was, however, largely recovered from, these securities

benefiting, like others, from the absence of competition, although a fresh cause of temporary
depreciation had set in, through the apprehension
of war in the East. In the same way, we may be
sure, there is a constant opposition of tendencies
in a market for securities when the shams are
being detected. The shocks cause great discredit,
and produce an immediate fall, but the market
for the remaining securities is permanently stronger
for the exposure.

The effect is not different in principle when a
security formerly of real value becomes a fictitious
security, such as when a mine unexpectedly gives
out. If such an event happened in a buoyant
time, and was not of itself big enough to turn the
tide of credit, it would have no appreciable influence. The rise of prices would go on with no
perceptible check, and equally without any perceptible fresh stimulus, the proportion of any one
such security to the whole market being infinitesimal. But such an event would certainly aggra-
vate the general discredit in a period of depression. It would be undistinguishable from the exposures of other securities, and would add to the
general confusion.

In all this, however, it must be carefully kept

in mind that we are speaking only of the money price. A temporary and partial depression of the price of securities, due to the shocks occasioned when sham securities are exposed, may be consistent with a real increase of value relatively to commodities, if the commodities are simultaneously falling in price for similar reasons. Such a fall in commodities is *quâ* commodities a rise in the price of securities, and an increase at the same time of the real value of the security itself, as the income from it has a greater purchasing power.

CHAPTER VIII.

THE MANNER OF STOCK EXCHANGE FLUCTUATIONS— PANICS.

WE have already pointed out that the organization of business on the Stock Exchange, and the methods pursued, are conducive to an incessant fluctuation, though within narrow limits, and to great liability to panics. To the outsider nothing can be more bewildering than these incessant ups and downs and great disturbances, for which there is apparently no assignable cause. But there is clearly nothing in them to modify the general rules we have laid down as to the causes of change in the price of securities and their effects. Experience of other affairs familiarises most men with the idea that frequent eddies in a current do not alter its general direction, which remains perfectly traceable, and that after great disturbances there are reactions which make the effect of the disturbances only temporary, and which are of little account when long periods are reckoned. There is so much interest, however, in Stock Exchange movements, that some account of the way in which these eddies and disturbances occur in this instance may perhaps be ventured on. Such an account will only confirm the view that they must operate within narrow limits, and leave the great movements in the prices of securities unaffected.

The constitution of the Stock Exchange is such that as a rule a great many transactions are entered into with borrowed money. As in most other markets, the dealers employ not only their own capital, but the money they can borrow from the banks in the operations of buying and selling. At the same time the solid nature of many of the securities, their slight liability to any great change in market price within short limits of time, their stable earning power, even if the market price should change, combine to enable the dealers on the Stock Exchange, on occasion, to borrow much more in proportion to their own capital than could be done in any other business. A large dealer in consols, to take an extreme illustration, might safely become responsible for an advance of hundreds of thousands on consols, with only a

one or two per cent margin, and almost with no
margin at all.   A bank could, of course, make the
advance with equal safety.   As the advances, by
the custom of the market, are also for short
periods, there is all the more safety in the operations, and the margin of the advance may be the
smaller.   There is also an additional security in
many of the operations from the known fact that
the dealer does not run the risk of fluctuation
even for the short period of the advance.   Say
he borrows of a bank to take up a quantity of
stock sold to him for cash, he may only want the
money for a few days until the usual settlement
comes round, for which settlement he may already
have sold the stock he has bought for cash.   If a
dealer is known to conduct his business prudently,
so that the sales he has made are not likely to
be the occasion of default by a purchaser, a banker
in lending to such a dealer has a very perfect
security, even if the entire advances are many
times in excess of the dealer's own capital.   There
are, no doubt, many securities where the advances by a prudent banker would be more
limited, and where dealers must be treated with
more caution ; but it is singular, I believe, with
what narrow margins, owing to the custom of

short settlements, advances are often made on very inferior securities.

This extreme borrowing will naturally have some effect in making markets sensitive. A dealer who may happen to hold a large amount of stock will be likely to start at shadows, and at any rate press sales, if he can do so at a small reduction only, so as to get out. He only borrows in the course of his ordinary business, and in anticipation of sales he is about to make; he does not contemplate a long speculation; he is therefore always apprehensive, and if there is a chance of things turning, and of anything happening which may leave stock he only means to deal in on his hand, or realisable only at an extraordinary loss, he hastens to anticipate so disastrous a contingency.

What we have described is in the ordinary way of a dealer's legitimate business, and might occur even in the absence of those Stock Exchange transactions which are more speculative, or where the gambling element comes in. But the extent of speculation, and the arrangements for it, also contribute to the general sensitiveness. The essence of these speculations is that outsiders, or brokers and dealers not in the ordinary way of

dealing but for speculation, enter into vast engagements precisely as the good dealer does, but
without the favouring conditions which make
him a tolerably safe borrower. As we have
explained, the usual stability of prices tempts
them. The outsiders are also without the dealer's
opportunities of turning round promptly, the
dealer's opportunity of doing so consisting in fact
in the steady stream of business which goes on
until an event occurs to change it, and in this
event being known sooner in the market than to
the multitude outside. The minor arrangements
also for this speculative dealing serve to conduce
to sensitiveness. Many purchases are made with
money which outsiders borrow directly of the
banks, but most are effected on the credit of the
buyer with his own broker, and on the latter's
credit with the dealer. When settling-day comes
round, the outside speculator, not being able to
pay for what he has bought, and not having
borrowed outside, gets his broker, as it is called,
to 'continue' the transaction—that is, as above
explained, to pay what is called a 'contango.' This
means that his broker either goes to the original
dealer and pays him a consideration for postponing
delivery and payment for the stock, or goes to an-

other dealer and pays him a consideration to take the stock if necessary. Sometimes it is said a broker receives such a consideration himself, but this would be contrary to formal rule, and is, moreover, a detail not necessary for our present purpose to be considered. Often also it happens that speculative purchases are set off against speculative sales, the rate of 'continuation' varying with the supply of stock, as it is called, as well as with the rate of discoun t ;but to each individual speculator the arrangement is in form, and may be for aught he knows in substance, an arrangement to borrow from some dealer or other to complete a purchase the speculator cannot himself complete. The borrowing is only for a short time—to the next settling day—that is, on the London Stock Exchange from a fortnight to three weeks ; but it is a real borrowing to the extent that there are no speculative sales to set against the speculative purchases. And the mere form of the borrowing is a perpetual cause of sensitiveness. The incessant renewal of loans acts, as a rule, unpleasantly on those who have to pay the charge, and at the approach of every account almost there is a cessation of active purchases, a disposition to sell, so as to avoid the renewal of the loan, and a vague uneasiness which results from comparing notes and the making of financial arrangements. Necessarily, also, each settling day reveals something as to the general state of the engagements —whether stock is in good supply or not, and so on ; and in excited times this revelation has a great effect on immediate prices.

The arrangements by which a supply of stock is kept about the markets seem also to ensure not only that the markets will be sensitive, but that they must be irregular. The essence of the business is that there should be floating stock in the market, unless when a great fall is anticipated, no matter in whose hands the stock may be. The outside speculation would otherwise have no raw material to work on. The dealers of all kinds will hold this stock when sales have been in excess of the current demand, or when prices from any cause have fallen below the usual average level at a given period. But when business again is active, and speculators are stirring, they sell the stock, not delivering it, but ' taking it in'—that is, receiving from borrowing buyers the ' continuations' we have described, or, in other words, lending the buyer the money represented by the market value of the stock. And as it is uncertain at what point in a rising market the various groups of dealers will sell, the result is that every rise is checked at uncertain intervals by this stock coming forward. The speculators for the rise may have the utmost confidence in their speculation, but they do not wish to be loaded with too much, unless the stock is small enough to be rigged to the degree of a corner; they prefer when too much comes forward to hang back a little, so as to get the assistance of the usual purchases which can be depended on in a rising market.* The knowledge of these irregularities also induces other speculators to realise from time to time, however confident they may be in the ultimate result of the speculation. A movement of prices upwards becomes jerky in consequence, a sudden rise for two or three days or weeks being followed by a decline almost to the point from which a start was made. For similar reasons a movement of prices downwards is also jerky. As stocks fall, the dealers in the floating stock buy in at varying intervals, and speculators also make temporary purchases against

---

* And when there is a rig on foot they *imitate* the course of a regular speculation for the rise. See *supra* on fictitious securities.

their speculative sales, though these sales will be resumed after a short spurt.

The rates of continuation or backwardation, it will be observed, have nothing to do with the intrinsic value of a security, or even with its position for a rise or fall. A low rate of continuation may sometimes mean only that one or more groups of speculators have not sold their stock, though a point or two's further advance may induce them to sell it. A backwardation may also be quite consistent with a preponderance of sales of stock for delivery. The arrangements are certainly calculated to facilitate deception, because a continuation has primarily the aspect of showing a necessity to borrow money to pay for stock, and a backwardation the aspect of a scarcity of stock, showing the necessity of an advance of price before a supply will come out.

The liability of such a market to panics will hardly require description. It is sensitive to every breath that blows, and when a whirlwind comes, or even an ordinary gale, there is great ruin. Almost all concerned—the dealers, whose transactions are regular, as well as the speculators of every description, are under immense engagements; and if any real cause occurs for a fall beyond a certain point, there is great loss to be faced even by the most prudent. No matter how confident any one may be in his calculation that a stock must rise in value, an actual fall beyond a certain limit throws him out. He may be wise to sell even on a falling market if there is a risk of a further fall—a risk about which there is often a great difficulty in judging. The question is not altogether one of the strength of a speculator. The element of time enters into every business transaction. Although, therefore, he may hope for profit ultimately in his speculation, in spite of the delay caused by a panic, he has to consider that if prices go down, and remain down for any length of time, he is debarred from other transactions in which he might make a profit. He fears, in fact, the temporary lock-up of his capital quite as much as the ultimate failure of the speculation in which he is engaged. A so-called strong speculator besides has often to consider the weakness of others. There may be a danger in many states of the market that, in spite of real circumstances favouring a rise which in time will have their due effect, the panic may be so great as to cause a serious lock-up of money to the strongest. Those who know the market best are aware of the frightful convulsions to which it is exposed, and act accordingly.

The hubbub is also likely to be aggravated up to a certain point by the manœuvres of the inside operators, who have been the first to get out. The more they have had an opportunity of operating with the current stream before the secret gets out, the weaker is the 'account' when the real causes for the fall disclose themselves—up to a point. It is the interest of the very people with whom only the outside speculators can close their transactions to put down the price as low as possible. Competition ensures that they will not go too far in this course, so that the markets are at bottom steadier than if the inside speculators were not prepared for the event, but this strength and steadiness are latent, and could hardly be the basis of action by an outside operator.

Of course panics are very different according to the circumstances in which they occur, although there is hardly ever a time except just after a panic when the stock-markets are not liable to great disturbance. Their normal condition is that large quantities of stock are held with borrowed money in various ways, and the *debacle* once set

in may go very far. At a point the stock which
has been pledged with banks for advances of
longer term than those customary on the Stock
Exchange itself is likely to be offered, and this
renders more hopeless the position of every one
who has made purchases with borrowed money.
The usual events which are likely to cause a
serious panic,—the outbreak of a sudden great
war, or a panic in the money-market,—are also
causes of a prolonged real change in the value of
securities about which every one may be justly
apprehensive. A really first-class war will be certain to cause a creation of securities on a large
scale. We know what has taken place in our own
great wars, and the more recent experience of the
United States and of France will be fresh in people's recollections. When war breaks out therefore, or is suddenly threatened, speculators know
for certain that an event is at hand which will
not only disturb the markets temporarily, but may
absolutely defeat their speculation. A large creation of securities, as we have seen, tends to lower
the price of every security, sometimes for a long
period. The outbreak of a great war is also like
the letting out of water of which no one can see
the end. We have been accustomed to think

G

from the experience of the last twenty years in Europe, that wars will be short, although the experience of the American civil war was quite of a contrary kind. But speculators will hardly count on this, and with reason. They see that some wars have been very short in which one side has displayed from the beginning a greatly preponderating force, and has been able to occupy the central resources of the enemy. It does not follow that a war in which some accident prevents this preponderance of force being felt, or in which a third power suddenly intervenes, will be at all short. If England had interfered in 1870 to prevent the final overthrow of France, it is quite possible that all Europe might still have been fighting just because we could have supplied France with an unassailable base. If an Eastern war should also break out in which England should be engaged, Europe might again be subjected to a prolonged struggle. Speculators justly fear, therefore, in every war, an indefinite creation of securities which completely upsets the calculation for the rise in which they are concerned.

A panic in the money-market is also likely to have the same effect. Such a panic means a great shock to credit which destroys the very condition

of a high level of price such as continued purchases with borrowed money bring about. It is
also one of those events which put in motion a
set of causes giving shock after shock to credit.
The speculator justly fears, therefore, that when
once such a panic sets in, there will be no quick
recovery in the markets for securities, but, on the
contrary, a slow decline succeeding the panic even
if at first it should be followed by a slight reaction.

But it is only in the way thus described that a
panic affects the great movements of prices. At
the time the depression, however great, usually
passes away leaving comparatively little mark.
Even in the case of the outbreak of a war there is
a recovery when the event is known, from the first
speculative depreciation, though not to the full
height from which the fall took place. It is only
after a time that the successive sales produced by
a shock to credit, or the competition of new issues
due to a war or other influences, produce their full
effect. It is not the panic mainly, but the circumstances in which it occurs and its indirect consequences to which the permanent change in prices
is to be traced.

CHAPTER IX.

THE DIFFERENCE OF PRICE OF SECURITIES, INTER SE.

IN a previous chapter we referred momentarily to the causes which make securities differ in price among themselves, although the aggregate price of the whole mass and the average yield obtainable upon investments are governed by the general causes we have stated. It may be convenient to describe some of the more important causes of difference of price among securities themselves apart from the rate of interest they pay, so that a greater nominal yield is obtainable from one than from another. There is a common impression that the differences are often wholly unaccountable, or are disproportionate to their real causes, which may frequently be the case ; but a proper consideration of the whole question may perhaps explain many apparent anomalies to those who have not fully reflected on the matter.

The *first* cause of difference we shall thus notice, is the difference in the security and safety of the income yielded by the investment. The obligations of the best governments are generally recognised as holding the first place, and with much good reason. The credit of a State is one of the most essential things to its life. The whole machinery of government in a state, and with that the due protection of its whole industry, must go wrong before the interest on the national obligations of the government, or the principal when due, can go unpaid. The whole fortune and industry of the subjects are in fact mortgaged for the payment of the government's debts. Hence the value of the obligations of stable governments of civilised communities, even when the debts of these governments may seem dangerously large. Whatever the danger they involve to the whole community, they are more secure than any other security possessed by that community. Of course there are various degrees of government credit, and a government which has to borrow from others than its own subjects cannot have the benefit of the preference of its own obligations to all other securities within the country which the governments of countries with much surplus capital

possess, but as regards the governments of first-
rate States, such as France, England, Germany,
and the United States, and of States like Holland
and Belgium, there are manifest reasons for the
common estimation of the solidity of their obligations.

There are other securities which tend to approach in value those of governments. As a State
advances materially, and the proportion of government securities to the resources of a country and
its other securities diminishes, there grows up a
mass of dividend-yielding investments which are
practically indistinguishable in point of solidity
from those of the government itself.   Of these
we may instance especially, among securities not
negotiable on the Stock Exchange, mortgages on
land or unimproved ground-rents, and some of the
obligations of local authorities which are based on
the security of rates ; and among securities which
are negotiable on the Stock Exchange, the debenture stocks of industrial undertakings, like the
chief English railways, where there is a very large
margin of net earnings. Theoretically these
things are not quite so solid as the obligations of
the English government itself. They are not the
first charge on the fortune and industry of the

country, or any part of it. Railway debenture stocks, again, are theoretically exposed to industrial fluctuations; railways *may* become antiquated or fall into a second place, like turnpike roads or canals. But the security of property in England is so great, that even second and third charges on the whole fortune and industry of the country are practically as good as the first. The English government must borrow hundreds and thousands of millions before the weight of the first charge would become such as materially to affect the security of the income of any other property in the country. The theoretical possibility of extreme fluctuations in industrial enterprises which would affect articles like railway debenture stocks may also be such as to have only an infinitesimal effect on market price. Still the theoretical notion being a *first* charge will probably have a powerful effect always in keeping a certain distance between government securities and others, even in the securest countries, other causes, as we shall see, being also likely to co-operate.

After the best securities come the obligations of all but the first-rate governments; the shares, whether preference or ordinary, in railways, gas-companies, banks, ships, and other undertakings, the variety being endless and the estimation most various. The only point to notice here is, perhaps, that some securities are affected by a positive drawback in the shape of an obligation contingent or otherwise. We refer to the shares of companies on which there is an uncalled liability. The consequent obligation is a most serious matter in almost every case, as may be seen in the price of the shares of the best Joint Stock Banks as compared with the leading railways, but the effect may vary from the comparatively slight degree in which it is manifested in such cases to the degree of giving a wholly *negative* price to the security, which the seller then pays something to be rid of. In the time of the 1866 collapse such payments to be rid of an investment were very common, and the risk at all times is never to be lost sight of. The prevalence of a form of securities on which there was a possible liability in a given country would probably have the effect of keeping the range of aggregate prices at a lower level than would otherwise be the case.

We may remark, however, generally, that it is very often the inferior security which is apt to be overvalued, and not the better security. The anxiety to enjoy a good income leads people to under-estimate the risks of an inferior security. When the account is taken after a period it will often be found that the investor in consols has really done better than an investor in a security yielding nominally a much higher interest, if the latter takes into account temporary losses or interruption of interest, and loss of capital, to which all investments are exposed. At the present time the investing public is in a position to be very sensible of this by their losses in Turkish, Egyptian, Peruvian, and similar securities.

A *second* cause of difference is the difference of marketability arising mainly from the greater mass of some securities than others, though it may be assisted by other causes. We have seen already that Stock Exchange securities are probably higher than others relatively, because of their susceptibility to accurate definition and subdivision, which makes them suitable for the handling of a great market. And what makes the mass of some Stock Exchange securities high in price will also make some of them higher than others; some of them will be far more marketable than others. That this is so is familiar on the Stock Exchange, many securities being, in fact, nominally quoted there which from various causes remain pretty much in the position of outside securities, owing to their possessing in so low a degree the marketable qualities. And the most valuable additional quality fitting an article for a good market, besides the capability of easy definition and subdivision, appears to be mass. A stock to be highly marketable, and even to make it safe to have dealings in it, must be large enough to make it worth the while of a great number of people to be interested in it. A dealer in a small stock can never be quite sure against being cornered; while as the market must be limited it is equally unsafe to calculate on being able to borrow on it. Hence the suitability of a great mass of stock like consols or French rentes for the operations of a great market. *Ceteris paribus* such stocks will stand higher than very similar stocks which are not in such masses. No doubt very small stocks may sometimes be subject to considerable dealings on the Stock Exchange, especially where such stocks are in close relation with larger masses of stock of a similar description. There are, for instance, several railway stocks such as the deferred ordinary stocks of the Great Northern, South Eastern, Brighton, and Sheffield Railway Companies, which are in close relation with other stocks of the same companies, and whose price will always be affected by comparison with that of the other stocks of these railways, or with the stocks of English railways generally. But it is recognised in the market, we believe, that the smallness of these stocks makes dealing far less safe in them than in the ordinary stock of the London and North Western Company for instance. Dealing is, in fact, only made possible by a disproportionate quantity of the stocks getting into the hands of dealers; and for this and other reasons they are subject to greater fluctuations than other stocks, and probably stand at a permanently lower level than if they could be held in great masses, although they may be occasionally higher in times of speculative inflation.

The above two are, we believe, the most important of the causes which make securities differ in price *inter se*, but they are not the only ones. There are other causes which may be occasionally important. We have to notice,—

Third, the effect of extrinsic regulations, such as those of law courts, which direct the investment and re-investment of funds in a particular manner, and so cause some stocks to be directly

more in demand besides giving them a certain
prestige.   Consols, English railway debentures,
and other stocks, are undoubtedly favoured by our
law courts in various degrees, with some effect
on the level of price of such securities.   The voice
of the courts of law makes them in effect articles
of luxury and monopoly to a certain extent, and
as compared with other securities the price is
likely to be raised accordingly.   It is just possible
that the judgment of the law courts may only anticipate the judgment of the public, nor is their
power unlimited, because while they divert some
capital in a particular direction they have not
power over all capital; but it is more probable
that an artificial cause of this sort will divert to
some extent, and in the direction of raising some
securities more than others, the natural currents
of investment.

Lastly, the estimation of the public may be
guided to some extent in favouring some securities
more than others by qualities unconnected with
the solidity of the income or mere marketability.
Securities, for instance, may be used, and are
used, as a *quasi* money, or in place of foreign bills
of exchange.   A merchant or banker in London
having money to pay in Paris may effect his

purpose quite as well by buying in London French Rentes or some other security negotiable on the Paris Bourse, and then reselling what he has bought in Paris. Instead of sending a bill of exchange to Paris he sends a bond of the French or some other government, or the obligations or shares of a railway company, like the Lombardo-Venetian railway. At times very considerable transactions of this nature do in fact take place. An exchange dealer who wants to send money from one capital to another, when there are no bills to be had, will buy securities in the one and send them to the other. The operation will probably be that he has sold drafts of his own to people who have inquired for them, and he finds the money to meet those drafts by the purchase and transmission of securities. One result is that when exchange is favourable to a country the demand is liable to be met by an exportation of securities to it, and *vice versâ*, and thus securities come to play an important part in regulating the exchanges, as it is called, and in equalising the rates for money in different monetary centres. But this secondary use of securities as money, like the secondary use of the precious metals themselves originally as money, tends to make more in demand the securities which are most suited for international transmission than probably they would otherwise be, or than securities which are not international. The bonds and shares of the Lombardo-Venetian Railway, to take a case already mentioned, probably enjoyed a special favour at one time, if not at present, for no other reason than the number of markets where they have been effectually domiciled, and the use for remittance which can thus be made of them.

Of the same nature is the extraneous value some securities come to acquire through their giving a status or some such advantage. It is, for instance, 'respectable' to hold bank stock, as giving an ownership in the national bank, and— the list of holders being published — as an indication of the wealth of the holder. No poor man can afford to hold bank stock: and important city firms who wish to have a partner in the bank direction, or to be in a certain kind of credit, will accordingly invest in bank stock when they would not otherwise do so. To a certain extent, I know, the better classes of railway and bank stocks are sought after for extrinsic advantages they are supposed to confer and will no doubt assist in conferring.

In addition, there is no doubt, I should think, from the peculiar value of some stocks, that there grows up at times a species of customary appreciation of which a distinct account can hardly be given. Custom, for instance, keeps Consols a half or three quarters per cent higher than New and Reduced Three per cents, although they pay exactly the same rate of interest and are indistinguishable in their legal conditions of value. The speculative 'account' is in consols by virtue of ancient custom, and for this and for no other reason, I am assured, Consols are always fractionally higher than New and Reduced. To take another illustration : A certain railway or bank comes to be a 'favourite.' It is first in the field or the first to be in very good credit ; all the best people go into it, and so it comes to enjoy a special repute and favour. This may sometimes be based at starting on a substantial reason. London and North Western Railway stock, for instance, has got to its present credit in part by the diffused belief in the rigour of the auditing, which has had for result that there would be a large real surplus if the Company were to relax the rigour it displays, as compared with other companies, in charging items of expense to revenue. But the benefit is participated in by many people who could not themselves appreciate all the reasons, and who simply follow the leader. It is the same to some extent with bank stock and other securities—a certain custom has attracted attention to them, and the opinion that they are generally thought well of keeps them in high credit.

These appear to be among the prominent causes of securities differing in value among themselves, and which may also modify a little the strictness of the relation between the price of securities and that of other commodities or the hire of money. Obviously, however, none of them are of a nature seriously to modify the rule that the expectation of income, as measured by what the income purchases —that is, the price of other commodities—*primarily* governs the estimation in which securities are held, or to modify the rules which make the fluctuations of price in the aggregate depend on the quantity of money on one side and the quantity of securities and commodities on the other, and also on the state of credit. The secondary qualities, such as the use of securities as money, could not be perceived or appreciated unless securities had first gained consideration from their primary qualities.

These causes of difference may seem so powerful as to be sufficient to isolate the different groups of securities—to put them, as it were, into water-tight compartments—so that what affects one should not much or quickly affect the others, and the general causes we have described should not be quickly or generally operative throughout the whole market. But reflection will make it clear that what is in fact the experience of the market—the sympathy between securities—is indeed quite reasonable. We have partly explained this already in con-nexion with the more speculative securities by a reference to the fact of speculators being banded together so that any loss to a part of the speculative class affects all the securities which the whole class holds. But there is another reason for the quick sympathy between securities, viz. what may be called the displacement of capital. It is not necessary that *all* the holders or possible holders of a particular security, or even all those who are about to buy or sell, should be affected by one or other of the influences favourable or adverse in order to produce a change in the level of price. If any of the holders are so affected, an apparently most disproportionate effect may be produced, so

H

that it will be the variable or optional capital which governs the price in the long run. It must be considered that there are constant operations of buying and selling in progress. Estates have to be realised, and for this and other reasons securities must be sold, although the sums realised have often to be immediately re-invested. In the same way money is always or almost always seeking investment. Consequently if a particular security or group of securities falls or rises in price, the optional capital will be attracted or repelled as the case may be; and the repulsion may sometimes go so far as to induce a certain part of the optional capital invested in a particular security to be realised. The diverted capital in turn seeking the securities to which it would be less naturally directed raises them to a price which diverts from them in a similar manner a part of their optional capital. And so it goes all through the market, this optional capital all through being the real harmoniser and adjuster of relative prices. Thus Consols may be usually sustained by the reinvestments of trustees, by the reinvestment of Savings Bank funds, and by a certain amount of customary purchasing; but if the price becomes higher than before relatively to other securities and the value of money, a portion of the capital set free by daily realisations, or by special realisations in view of the high price, will go elsewhere, and new capital which would otherwise have been destined for Consols will also go elsewhere. A certain support will thus be taken from the consol market at a relatively high price which will only return to it when the diverted capital has exerted a disproportionate effect in raising other prices. This is what we mean by the displacement of capital, which is obviously a marvellous agency in the adjustment of prices.

One important result of this displacement may be noticed—viz., that certain special causes tending to raise the price of a security, instead of having all the effect they would have if other things remained the same, have mainly for effect to change the character of the holding. A particular security instead of being held by classes of capitalists in certain proportions will come to be held by other classes or by a portion of the former holders mixed with others in different proportions. Just as suddenly arrested motion evolves a certain amount of heat, so the force of the causes tending to raise prices being neutralised by other causes operates a change in the character of the holding. In the

case of Consols supposed the diminution of the
optional capital invested will leave a larger proportion than before held by trustees and others
who are bound to reinvest. In the case of inferior
securities it is believed this probable change in the
character of the holding with every great change
of price must often be an important matter. The
change may be so great as often to make the entire
difference between a security which is well held
and one which is badly held, or *vice versâ*. Its
whole relation to other securities, and its characteristics of marketability and stability, may be
profoundly altered—for good as well as for evil in
an investing point of view—as the result of a
change in the level of price. The sympathy
between securities, notwithstanding the distinc-
tions between them, appears thus the more extended and to have more and more important
consequences the more we look into their relations.
They are acted on by special influences of every
description, but there are constant forces at work
to restore an equilibrium based on a clear appreciation of their relative intrinsic qualities. There
can be no doubt also that where general causes
affect first a particular security or group of securities, the ready sympathy between all secures the

quickly diffused operation of such general causes. Hence in part the simultaneous movements in many securities which cannot but strike observers as one of the remarkable characteristics of the Stock Exchange.

CHAPTER X.

THE CYCLE OF PRICES IN SECURITIES.

In a previous chapter we have referred to the probability that the prices of securities will tend to move in great waves—that they will in the aggregate be constantly advancing for a long period, and then for another long period will be almost constantly declining. This effect results from the constitution of human nature dealing with such articles as we have described in the actual conditions of business. Although at first sight a rise in one security would mean a depreciation of all others, if the quantity of money was not simultaneously increased, yet the effect of credit and of other causes is such as to make other securities in the first instance rise in sympathy with the movement, and continue rising, the competition for the limited amount of money being only felt at a later stage in the advance.

The point is so important that a more ample discussion of it may be useful.

That there is ordinarily a cycle in all prices such as we have described may now be considered an established doctrine in Political Economy. Several acknowledged authorities have given their opinion to this effect, and have also collected a mass of substantial evidence in its favour. I would instance especially Mr. Tooke in his *History of Prices*. In the long discussions of that book, which were so ably continued down to 1856 by Mr. Newmarch, and have since been continued in the Annual Commercial History and Review of the *Economist*, nothing is more striking than the periodicity of prices. At one period the range of prices of all or of the majority of the principal articles is much lower than it was a year or two before. This lasts for a few years, or a longer or shorter interval as the case may be, loud complaints of dulness and depression being heard all the while from the mercantile classes. Then all the prices begin to rise one after another and quickly participate in a general ascending movement, now most marked in one article and now in another, till finally a high range of prices is established, coupled with a feeling of great cheerfulness in trade and an impression of general prosperity. This high range of prices lasts for a certain period, and then comes a re-descent to the level or something like the level from which they rose, accompanied probably by successive failures, great excitement in the money market, and the collapse on all sides of every species of financing. All this Mr. Tooke and his successors have shown during a period extending from the close of last century to the present time, the evidence being the more valuable from its being adduced at first incidentally to support conclusions as to the effect of bank-note circulation on prices, and *vice versâ*. There is also a French authority on the subject of very great weight—M. Clement Juglar, whose able book on *Crises Commerciales* deals not only with the commercial cycle in England, but extends our range of view to other Continental countries and the United States, showing the universality of the causes at work and their deep root in human nature. Another authority is Professor Stanley Jevons, who shows in his book on the gold discoveries and their effect on prices the necessity of disregarding or allowing for the cyclical changes so as to bring out the more permanent changes which may be considered attributable to the gold discoveries. More recently Mr. Bagehot in his *Lombard Street* has given his suffrage for the same view, supporting it by a special reference to the remarkable rise of prices in 1869–71. Mr. Bagehot's special object was to explain the periodical excitement of the money market, but his evidence consists mainly of the great movement of prices.

Mr. Bagehot's explanation of the reason of the cycle generally appears also a sufficient one. His theory is, that a cycle of prosperity begins by something happening to favour a particular trade. Something occurs to make the products of that trade greatly in demand ; all those who are in it make greater profits than before ; these profits make them stronger and larger purchasers from other trades, which in turn become more profitable, and so by action and reaction trades A, B, C, and D, and so on, all through the letters of the alphabet, are stimulated and re-stimulated. Usually, Mr. Bagehot thought, it is the great textile trades which feel the stimulus first, that stimulus coming to them from a long period of cheap food, which enables the masses of labourers to spend more on other articles than food ; but probably this element has for many years in England been less important than it used to be in the commencement of a cycle of prosperity, because the masses of our workmen have usually a much larger margin than formerly for other articles than food, and the changes in the price of wheat, since the free-trade period began, have been much less extreme than they were when the dependence of commercial prosperity on cheap food was noticed. Still there is no doubt that a cycle of prosperity does seem to arise out of a period of generally low prices, and its foundations are laid in these prices which cannot but have the effect, as we have seen, of raising the real yield of securities, and of increasing the command of the capitalists who hold securities over commodities. I should be inclined also to add to Mr. Bagehot's explanation of trades becoming successively profitable, the fact that these profits are very often merely paper profits, and are thus the direct creation of a changed state of credit. Mr. Bagehot was too well aware of the effect of credit on business to overlook its effects, but he seemed to consider most the influence it had in stimulating production, and so increasing the quantity of things produced; that is, the real wealth of a community. But its effect in raising nominal prices, and so making profits appear large, seems

to me quite as important, and to explain most
the facility with which a change from a low to
a high level of prices is effected. The increase
of production is, *pro tanto*, an influence acting
in the direction opposite to a rise of prices, and
when a really large increase begins, or the means
for that production are greatly increased, which is
the final result of a rise of prices, the influence
is at once manifest in a quick fall. It is the rise
in nominal prices, therefore, causing merely paper
profits and an appearance of wealth, which is for
the present purpose the most remarkable characteristic of the prosperity period in a commercial cycle. In other words, people have more
courage then than at other times, and trade A,
say, is made good, because B, C, D, and all the
other letters of the alphabet, speculate more,
begin to hold stocks of larger nominal value, and
so swell the deposits in the banks without any
proportionate increase in the quantity of articles.
In the same way the characteristic of the depressed period is a failure of this credit element,
and a reduction of prices, consequently a reduction of the apparent wealth of many people,
without any corresponding reduction of the real
wealth of the community.

Such is the cause and explanation of a cycle of prices generally. Dealing more particularly with securities, we should say there are various reasons deducible from the general principles set forth in previous chapters why they should be among the things specially and strongly acted upon, first in the upward, and then in the downward direction.

The extreme marketability of securities is one reason—and a principal one—why they should be quickly affected. When all prices are liable to be affected from certain causes, that is, when certain common motives of mankind are likely to cause an excess of demand over the supply of all articles on the one side, or an excess of supply over demand on the other, it is articles subject to speculative manipulation of which the offer or demand is likely to be most in excess, and in which therefore there will be the readiest movement in prices. The disposition to buy or sell, which is, *ex hypothesi*, a general one, and not specially appropriated to particular articles, moves like other forces along the lines of least resistance, and there is obviously less resistance in the speculative markets than in others. The markets are speculative, because of the facilities they afford to buying and selling, their adaptability to speculation in turn largely making the facilities. Transactions in them can be entered into at once on a large scale, and every one who buys and sells is assured of being able to effect the counter operation, in which his hope of profit, or of avoiding great loss, rests. Markets where buyers have to find sellers, and sellers to find buyers, or where from the nature of the articles dealt in there is only a hand-to-mouth trade, have no chance against the more refined ones, and prices in them accordingly move less orderly, although they are subject to greater extremes.

The above is a general reason, applicable to all speculative articles, why securities should participate greatly in the upward and downward movements of prices, but there are also special causes peculiar to securities — some helping to raise them in good times, and others helping to depress them in bad times. Of the former we notice, first, that the creation of surplus profits, which is the characteristic of a period of prosperity, produces a demand for investments. The profits may be only paper profits, still a certain number of those who have made them immediately wish to invest, so as to earn an interest on their new capital. Partly in conse-

quence of this the speculation of the period is
specially attracted to securities. That the fact is
so is peculiarly shown by another feature of a
prosperity period—the great demand for such
articles as coal and iron. To meet the demand
for investments, new works are embarked on, and
in these new works iron plays a principal part,
so that iron, and with it coal, come largely into
demand. The resulting revival of the coal and
iron industries in turn swells the general prosperity, though the enhancement of price ensuing
becomes again a primary cause of the general un-
profitableness of industry and of a reaction
towards a low level of prices. But the fact of
an increased demand for coal and iron from the
cause we have stated is unquestionable, and is the
sign of a special cause at work operating to raise
the price of securities.

Secondly, the surplus profits created in a
period of prosperity are of a kind likely to take
the shape of deposits in banks. They are profits
rather in excess of the normal or average
rate of profit. It must not be supposed that
in what are called bad years there are losses in
every trade. On the contrary, profits are made
in many trades, perhaps not much in excess of

what is needed to reward the skill and industry applied in the conduct of the trade, but still sufficient to provide a fund for extensions and improvements ; and even it may be to a moderate extent for other new investments. But when good times come, there is immediately an excess of profit, for which there is no immediate outlet through the usual channels. It is probably the result of the purchases of speculators who have borrowed of a bank for the purpose, and there is not likely to be any large excess of profit without such borrowing. But whatever the origin, as there is no outlet for it, it remains deposited with the banks until an outlet can be found. In this shape it will be sure to act in two ways on securities; first, directly by providing a fund which comes into the Stock Exchange for direct investment; and secondly, a fund which may be, and is, lent to speculators in various ways through the medium of banks. There is a special connexion between banks and the markets for securities which diverts banking money to the Stock Exchange. Bankers are accustomed to handle securities which bear interest, and they form judgments of their own about the more prominent in the market. They also prefer them as pledges to warrants for cotton, corn, and the like, because of their bearing interest. The want of this quality in ordinary commodities which have been pledged as security for an advance will often cause bankers to precipitate their realisation, when a security bearing interest would be held for a more suitable time to realise.

Thirdly, in a time of prosperity, when speculators make money, and are on the outlook for new speculations, they are apt to be tempted by securities of an inferior description nominally yielding a high interest. On these they borrow at a low rate of interest, and pocket the difference between that and the high rate yielded by the security itself, while also profiting, or hoping to profit, by the rise in price which they anticipate at such a time. There is a double profit, as it were. Hence speculators are as eager to use the facilities offered by bankers, as bankers are tempted, from the causes above mentioned, to afford them. It is well known that in the period preceding the foreign loan collapse, securities like Turkish, Peruvian, and Egyptian, were largely held for long periods by speculators, who counted on the difference of interest. The game is a most risky one, as the event has proved, but we have only to deal here with the fact that this cause, among others, tends to raise securities disproportionately when all prices are going up.

Fourthly, the fact that securities in a time of low prices generally really yield more than at other times is no doubt a cause for bringing them quickly into favour at such times, and diverting to them both purchases for investment and speculation. We should not say that it is a very important cause, as it must work obscurely, and does not supply a direct and palpable motive for ordinary people to act upon; but it can hardly fail to have some effect.

These are all reasons in the nature of securities why they should specially advance in an upward movement of prices; and just because they have specially advanced, they will decline when the current turns. The reaction will naturally be manifest where the previous action has been most felt. Other special reasons for securities sharing in the decline may, however, be given, such reasons being mainly the reverse of those which we have assigned specially for the rise of securities in good times.

First. There is not only, when prices fall, a

I

disappearance of the paper profits which seek the
markets for investment, but there is a substitution
for them of paper losses which in various ways
forces the realisation of investments.   Prices generally having reached a maximum, the changes
which occur begin to be downwards, and this
means a loss to all holders.   Were there no borrowers in the world, such losses might have no
very serious consequences.   To a large extent
they would mean that capitalists had to write
themselves nominally poorer than before, but their
real wealth, that is, the exchangeability of what
they possessed for other things, would be unaffected.   But the rise of prices, as we have seen,
having been due to borrowing, and the stocks of
articles being held by people who have only an
interest in the margin of value above what they
have borrowed, a great fall of prices means a
change of conditions forcing them to realise their
loss.   They have to sell the articles pledged to
pay their creditor, or the creditor sometimes forces
a sale, if the debtor does not voluntarily act.
Instead of a surplus of profits, therefore, seeking
investment, which is the characteristic of a period
of prosperity, there is a positive loss, which rather
takes the direction of a realisation of the articles

in which investment is made, that is, of securities.
In course of time there is a large class of people
who have losses to meet, and if they have securities to sell they sell them.   Many of the class, it
is plain, must have securities to sell.   They have
been swayed by the attractions to speculate in
securities offered in the prosperous period, and
securities are consequently among the things they
can realise.

The real wealth of a community as a whole
will not, of course, be changed proportionally by
the realisation of such paper losses, although
perhaps there can be no large realisation of paper
losses without the pre-existence of conditions
diminishing real profits.   But the paper losses
so called are of course material to those who
suffer them, and contribute much to that change
in the state of credit which accompanies and promotes a change from a high to a low level of
prices.

Secondly. Securities are specially affected by
the diminution of the deposits of banks, which
contribute so much, as we have seen, to the rise in
prices.   These deposits are themselves in part the
creation of speculation of every sort, and particularly speculation in securities.   Profits being

above the normal amount, those who realised them, not being able to employ them in the usual outlets, left them at the banks, who have a strong disposition and many motives to employ them on the Stock Exchange. But when surplus profits are not made, and losses have to be met, these deposits in the bank must diminish. There is no other fund out of which to meet the losses. To take the most favourable case of a solvent speculator whose margin has run off, and more than run off. What happens, when his security is realised, is, that having borrowed say 8000*l.* on what was supposed to be worth 10,000*l.*, on which therefore there was a margin of 2000*l.*, and the security in fact realising only 6000*l.*, he has to find 2000*l.*, besides losing all his margin. If he has 2000*l.* deposited with the banker of whom he borrowed, his individual deposit would be diminished by so much, and there would be no increase of deposits in any other direction. The amount realised by the security and the 2000*l.* would all go to meet the debt due to the bank, which would be extinguished—the result of the operation as regards the 2000*l.* being in fact a diminution of the loans of the banks on one side, and of their deposits on the other. The result would be the same if the

speculator had been insolvent, and the bank had
had to meet the loss—it would have had so much
to write off the credit to profit and loss, which
counts as part of the deposits, instead of to the
credit of an individual customer. Operations like
this going on with a great mass of speculation, it
is quite intelligible how the deposits in the banks
may steadily diminish for a time merely through
a fall in the nominal price of articles. It is not
that the community as a whole is poorer, but
some people are, and the poverty takes the shape
of diminishing a fund which helps much, as we
have seen, to inflate securities when all prices are
rising.

We need not point out how the withdrawal of
such a fund must affect securities. At the very
time speculators are suffering from their own
losses, and the temptations to speculate are otherwise diminished, the fund upon which the whole
speculation rests is curtailed or disappears.
Bankers, it is found, throw the pawned stock
they have on the markets, and call in the advances they have made on the Stock Exchange.
They have no option. Their deposits are being
drawn on to meet losses, and they have no longer
a surplus to lend.

A very good illustration of the peculiar effect of this withdrawal from the Stock Exchange in consequence of the diminution of banking deposits was given, I think, at the close of 1875 and the spring of 1876. The year 1875 had witnessed a great commercial collapse succeeding a great fall in the prices of almost all articles, and accompanied by a great fall in securities, especially those of foreign governments, which culminated in the autumn of 1875. Nothing seemed more remarkable for a long period than the way in which the Stock Exchange securities not directly affected by this collapse bore up and even advanced. But the events had been such as to cause a diminution of banking deposits; the banks throughout the country became poor instead of having a surplus; and early in 1876 the result was manifest in extensive realisations of English railway securities, which had at first rather benefited by the great collapse of the competing foreign securities. The diminution of banking deposits was thus found to be powerful enough to neutralise other influences promoting a rise in some securities. No doubt the consequent fall in English railway securities illustrates to some extent as well the underlying sympathy between great groups of securities, as has been already noticed in the chapter on fictitious securities. But the poverty of the banks was so much spoken of at the time, as contributing to the withdrawals of money from the Stock Exchange, that the facts seem worthy of notice also in the present connexion.

Thirdly. The fall in securities from a high level is of course promoted by the opposite of what promotes their rise from a low level, viz. the diminished yield of the security at the high price. As in the case of a rise through the increased yield of securities when prices are low, we doubt if this cause is ever conspicuously operative; but it cannot but govern men's motives to some extent. It is one among other reasons which make people distrust the maintenance of prices which have recently advanced greatly. So far as it goes, it furnishes a special reason for the decline of the price of securities when the period of adversity in the commercial cycle and of the return to low prices begins.

Fourthly. The depreciation or collapse of many fictitious securities, when discredit sets in, will naturally affect almost all the markets for securities. The creation of such securities is one of the forms of inflation in prosperous times, and in the long run checks the rise which would otherwise take place in the better securities ; but their having been called into existence undoubtedly assists the reaction which afterwards comes. Nothing is so apt to create distrust than the discovery that many so-called securities are rubbish, and have no real value. In the end the removal of these bad securities out of the way will help the other markets ; but the first effect of the removal is to make the whole market more sensitive, and to hasten the change from a high to a low level.

We conclude, then, that securities are among the articles which will be specially acted upon by the causes promoting a general upward movement of prices, and also by the causes promoting a general downward movement. As a rule they will be quick to move, and within the limits imposed by the nature of the securities themselves the movements will be extreme. The opposite sets of causes being put in motion, there will be no rest in the movement until the extremes are touched. It will be understood, however, that this liability to movement will be quite consistent with comparatively narrow limits of variation in many cases as compared with other articles. The

value of securities being governed so largely by
the value of money, and many of them, especially
of the steady class, being only affected in a minor
degree by speculation and changes in the state
of credit, the extremes of high and low price
between which such securities will oscillate will
not be wide. It is obvious indeed, that while we
have spoken of the aggregate of securities as
being liable to great change in the level of price,
there must be a considerable class in which, with
great sensitiveness to causes of variation, there is
really great stability of price. The great variation
in the aggregate must, therefore, be due to excessive variations in other securities not of the better
class.

This last conclusion quite confirms the observations of the market. It is in the inferior securities that the causes of variation we have described
operate most. It is to them that speculation is
attracted when times are good, and to which
surplus profits, whether paper or genuine, are
diverted. Not only are fictitious securities created
ad hoc to use up the loose money about, but
doubtful enterprises are embarked in, resulting
in the creation of inferior securities which are
only not wholly fictitious. For special reasons

also securities bearing high interest are sought after by investors and speculators. It is again among such securities that there is collapse from real causes when the tide turns, and from which speculation is then withdrawn. Hence there is a large group of securities in which the movement from a low to a high level, and *vice versâ*, is not only rapid but enormous, so that the changes in a rise seem almost from no value at all to an immense sum, and then, when the opposite changes occur, the appearances· are like the complete destruction of an immense mass of property. As we have explained, it is almost all a paper change : it is only nominal values that are in question ; but these considerations are not felt at the time. The impression is made on the public mind that there is something specially intangible in securities, and that they are unlike all other articles, whereas in reality nothing is steadier than the better security, and it is in the inferior and sham article that excessive fluctuations occur. Great changes are to be looked for in the cycle of prices in securities, and even the best are sensitive, but the difference in the intrinsic qualities of the securities themselves is in this respect all-important.

CHAPTER XI.

ILLUSTRATIONS :—HAVE SECURITIES RISEN OR FALLEN IN RECENT YEARS ?

THE inquiry in some of the preceding chapters has led us to results for the most part of a negative character. However important Stock Exchange practices may be, however much they may affect particular securities or groups of securities for a time, and whatever indirect consequences panics may have as producing or aggravating that discredit which we have described as one of the most powerful influences on prices, they do not disturb the general relations of the price of Stock Exchange securities to that of other securities, or other articles, or to the value of money. They alter mainly, and for a time, the relations of particular groups of securities among themselves, but they are of such a nature that they can have no further influence. The only permanent effect the Stock Exchange appears to have, is that of making Stock Exchange securities higher in price than others through their being more saleable, and their suitability to perform the functions of money, and this effect is always operative. There is also a cyclical change of aggregate price both of securities and of other articles from one period to another, which must be distinguished from changes due to more permanent causes. If we would appreciate the lasting variations in securities, therefore, that is allowing for minor changes of a temporary character, and for changes in the relations of securities *inter se*, as well as the cyclical changes from a credit to a non-credit level of prices, and *vice versâ*, we must endeavour to deal with the facts in such a way as to eliminate these minor and cyclical changes; embrace the ranges of price over a long period of time; and compare the changes which may then be made apparent with similar changes in the price of commodities, and of other securities, and in the value of money.

We propose to deal, by way of illustration, with the changes of price in England since the free-trade period. Have securities as a mass risen or fallen in price in that period? and to which of the

main causes influencing price is the change, if any,
due ?

To answer such questions exactly, it would
be necessary to take account of many things
of which, it is plain, no exact account is possible.
It would be, for instance, impossible to state
exactly at any given time the exchangeable
value of the mass of Stock Exchange securities
in existence. The obstacles to such an account
would not only be the mere difficulty of ascertaining and counting the different sorts of
securities, but there would also be the difficulty of reckoning at certain times the masses
of securities which were afterwards discovered to
be fictitious, and of estimating at all times the
real yield of many securities, such as the shares in
public companies on which there are fluctuating
dividends. In addition, even if such an account
could be framed for this country, there would fall
to be considered the case of those international
securities which are dealt in on many markets, and
whose presence in greater or less quantity on the
home market will variously affect prices. All this
makes an account of quantities of securities and
their yield all but, if not quite, impossible ; but yet
it could only be shown by such an account what is

the average yield on securities at different times, which would be the only real test of a difference of aggregate prices. And even if the average yield at different times could be stated, this would only be a test of nominal price. There would remain the further question of whether there was, or was not, a corresponding change in real prices, in consequence of the average fall or rise in articles of general consumption. All these difficulties make an exact answer to the question put impossible, and we must be content with a rough approximation. We assume that the course of prices in certain leading securities will be a sufficient test of the general course of the market; and if this course agrees with the changes we should expect in accordance with it in the value of money or the price of other securities, we may be tolerably confident that a more exact account of securities and their yield from time to time would have led to a very similar conclusion.

The most familiar masses of securities are the obligations of governments, and the debentures and shares of the great railway companies, the latter being mainly the creation of the last thirty years. Of the former we propose to take as our type Consols, which have not increased in quan-

Table showing the average annual price of Consols in each year since 1844, as given in the Statistical Abstract, and the price of London and North Western Ordinary Stock in the last week of December in each year since 1848, and of Debenture and Preference Stocks of the same Railway since 1866; together with the yield to the investor at each price, the yield on North Western Ordinary Stock being calculated on the mean of the two nearest annual dividends.

Year.	Consols.		London and North Western 4 per cent. Debenture Stock.		London & Nth. Wstn. Railwy. 5 per cent. Preference Stock.		London and North Western Railway Ordinary Shares.		
	Price.	Yield to Investor.	Price.	Yield to Investor.	Price.	Yield to Investor.	Average Price.	Dividend for Year.	Yield to Investor.
1846	95	$3\frac{1}{8}$							
1847	$86\frac{1}{4}$	$3\frac{1}{2}$							
1848	$85\frac{1}{4}$	$3\frac{1}{2}$					127	7	$5\frac{1}{2}$
1849	$92\frac{1}{4}$	$3\frac{1}{2}$					124	6	$4\frac{3}{4}$
1850	$96\frac{1}{4}$	$3\frac{3}{8}$					114	$5\frac{1}{4}$	$4\frac{11}{16}$
1851	$96\frac{7}{8}$	$3\frac{3}{8}$					123	$5\frac{1}{4}$	$4\frac{1}{4}$
1852	$99\frac{1}{2}$	3					125	$5\frac{1}{4}$	$4\frac{7}{8}$
1853	$98\frac{1}{4}$	$3\frac{1}{16}$					112	5	$4\frac{7}{16}$
1854	$91\frac{1}{2}$	$3\frac{3}{4}$					$98\frac{1}{2}$	5	$5\frac{1}{16}$
1855	$90\frac{1}{4}$	$3\frac{3}{8}$					98	5	$5\frac{1}{16}$
1856	$93\frac{1}{8}$	$3\frac{1}{4}$					102	$5\frac{1}{2}$	$5\frac{3}{8}$
1857	$91\frac{7}{8}$	$3\frac{1}{4}$					101	5	5
1858	$96\frac{7}{8}$	$3\frac{3}{8}$					95	4	$4\frac{3}{16}$
1859	$95\frac{1}{8}$	$3\frac{3}{8}$					91	$4\frac{1}{2}$	5
1860	94	$3\frac{3}{8}$					101	$5\frac{1}{8}$	$5\frac{1}{16}$
1861	$91\frac{1}{2}$	$3\frac{1}{4}$					96	$4\frac{3}{4}$	$4\frac{7}{16}$
1862	93	$3\frac{1}{4}$					95	$4\frac{5}{8}$	5
1863	$92\frac{5}{8}$	$3\frac{1}{4}$					102	$5\frac{5}{8}$	5
1864	$90\frac{1}{2}$	$3\frac{3}{8}$					114	$6\frac{1}{4}$	$5\frac{9}{16}$
1865	$89\frac{1}{4}$	$3\frac{3}{8}$	97	$4\frac{1}{8}$			121	$6\frac{1}{4}$	$5\frac{9}{16}$
1866	88	$3\frac{3}{8}$	93	$4\frac{1}{4}$	106	$4\frac{3}{4}$	120	$6\frac{1}{4}$	$5\frac{5}{8}$
1867	93	$3\frac{1}{4}$	$96\frac{1}{4}$	$4\frac{1}{8}$	109	$4\frac{1}{2}$	117	6	$5\frac{1}{8}$
1868	$93\frac{7}{8}$	$3\frac{1}{4}$	$98\frac{1}{4}$	$4\frac{1}{16}$	$109\frac{1}{2}$	$4\frac{1}{2}$	116	6	$5\frac{3}{16}$
1869	$92\frac{7}{8}$	$3\frac{1}{4}$	101	4	$111\frac{1}{4}$	$4\frac{7}{16}$	118	$6\frac{1}{4}$	$5\frac{1}{4}$
1870	$92\frac{1}{4}$	$3\frac{1}{4}$	100	4	112	$4\frac{7}{16}$	126	$6\frac{5}{8}$	$5\frac{1}{16}$
1871	$92\frac{3}{4}$	$3\frac{1}{4}$	$101\frac{1}{2}$	$3\frac{15}{16}$	116	$4\frac{5}{16}$	142	$7\frac{3}{4}$	$5\frac{7}{16}$
1872	$92\frac{1}{4}$	$3\frac{1}{4}$	$103\frac{1}{4}$	$3\frac{7}{8}$	116	$4\frac{5}{16}$	151	$7\frac{1}{4}$	$5\frac{5}{8}$
1873	$92\frac{1}{2}$	$3\frac{1}{4}$	103	$3\frac{7}{8}$	117	$4\frac{1}{4}$	148	$7\frac{1}{4}$	$5\frac{1}{16}$
1874	$92\frac{1}{2}$	$3\frac{1}{4}$	104	$3\frac{7}{8}$	120	$4\frac{1}{8}$	149	$6\frac{7}{8}$	$4\frac{7}{8}$
1875	$93\frac{3}{4}$	$3\frac{1}{4}$	106	$3\frac{3}{4}$	$122\frac{1}{2}$	$4\frac{1}{16}$	146	$6\frac{1}{4}$	$4\frac{7}{8}$
1876	$95\frac{1}{4}$	$3\frac{1}{8}$	$107\frac{1}{2}$	$3\frac{3}{4}$	126	4	142	$6\frac{1}{4}$	$4\frac{7}{8}$

tity in the period, and of the latter we select the debentures preference stocks, and ordinary shares of the London and North Western Railway which is a typical English railway.   On the previous page (p. 127) is a table showing the price of Consols and average yield to investors in each year since 1846 inclusive; the price of London and North Western Railway shares and average yield to investors in each year since 1848 inclusive; and the price and average yield to investors of certain debenture stocks and preference shares of the latter company since 1866.   I should have liked in the case of the debenture stocks and preference shares to go back to some date before 1850, but debenture stocks are of comparatively recent origin, and the changes in the amount and position of different classes of preference shares are such that I found this course impracticable.   Still the figures as far as they go appear to tell a consistent tale.

Summarising the results as regards Consols and London and North Western Ordinary Stock for periods of five years as near as possible, we obtain the following comparison :—

Average yield of Consols and London and North Western Railway Ordinary Stock, in the following periods.

Period.	Yield of Consols.			Yield of London and North Western Ordinary Stock.		
	£	s.	d.	£	s.	d.
1846–50	3	6	0	5	0	0
1851–55	3	3	4	4	13	4
1856–60	3	3	4	4	18	6
1861–65	3	6	0	5	2	6
1868–70	3	5	0	5	3	9
1871–75	3	5	0	4	19	6
1876	3	2	6	4	12	6

From this table it is evident that if the movements in securities generally have at all corresponded with these examples, there was first a low price giving a large nominal yield immediately after the beginning of the free-trade period, then a rise in price accompanied by a less nominal yield lasting during the following decade, then a fall in price in 1861–65 — since which period there has been a steady rise to a point already higher, or about as high as any touched since 1846. Since 1866 also the movements in the debenture stocks and preference shares of the

K

railway have fully corresponded. The average yield of the debenture stock in 1866-70 was 5*l.* 1*s.* 9*d.*, in 1871-5 it was 3*l.* 17*s.* 6*d.*, and in 1876 it is only 3*l.* 15*s.* The average yield of the preference shares in 1866-70 was 4*l.* 10*s.* 6*d.* ; in 1871-5 it was 4*l.* 4*s.* 3*d.* ; and in 1876 it is only 4 per cent. The suggestion lies on the surface that the high yield of securities at the commencement of this period corresponded to the great creation of securities in 1845 and 1846 as the result of the railway mania; that the low yield in 1851-55 corresponded to the gold discoveries, but there was a tendency in the latter part of the decade 1851-60 to a higher yield, as is shown especially in the yield of London and North Western Ordinary Stock; that the high yield of 1861-65 corresponded to another large creation of securities in connexion with limited companies and contractors' railways ; and that the falling yield since 1865 probably indicates a period of less active creation of securities in comparison with the capital seeking investment. It is obvious from an inspection of the table that no such illustrations can be perfect, for the non-increase in quantity of Consols is a special cause for their improvement in value of the first magnitude, while the improvement in railway quotations may arise largely from a special improvement of the credit of railway companies, by which other securities have proportionally suffered. The masses dealt with are, however, so large that the illustration may perhaps pass as the best attainable.

It would complete the illustration if we could add a similar account of the chief foreign government securities, but to do so it would be needful to take account of so many complicated circumstances and changes in the stocks themselves, that we must limit ourselves to one or two stocks, whose history can be followed for a long period. The stocks we find most convenient are the French 3 per cents, and Russian 5 per cent 1822, whose history is detailed in the table on the following page (p. 132).

Here there have been greater fluctuations than in the first case, no doubt for political reasons. The high yield of French rentes in 1848–50 was partly a result of the political insecurity of those years, while the high yield of Russian stock in 1876 is of course the direct effect of the war on which Russia has embarked, and Russian stocks have also been affected all through, first, by the Crimean war, and its direct and indirect effects,

Table showing the annual price of the undermentioned Foreign Stocks, the last week of December in each year since 1844, together with the yield to the investor at each price.

Year.	French 3 per cent.		Russian 5 per cent 1822.	
	Price.	Yield to Investor.	Price.	Yield to Investor.
1846	$80\frac{3}{4}$	$3\frac{1}{8}$	111	$4\frac{1}{2}$
1847	$75\frac{5}{8}$	4	107	$4\frac{5}{8}$
1848	$46\frac{1}{8}$	$6\frac{7}{16}$	102	$4\frac{7}{8}$
1849	$56\frac{1}{8}$	$5\frac{5}{16}$	110	$4\frac{1}{2}$
1850	$57\frac{3}{4}$	$5\frac{3}{16}$	$110\frac{3}{4}$	$4\frac{1}{2}$
1851	66	$4\frac{3}{8}$	113	$4\frac{7}{16}$
1852	$82\frac{3}{4}$	$3\frac{5}{8}$	120	$4\frac{1}{8}$
1853	$74\frac{1}{4}$	4	112	$4\frac{7}{16}$
1854	68	$4\frac{3}{8}$	98	$5\frac{1}{8}$
1855	$64\frac{1}{4}$	$4\frac{5}{8}$	96	$5\frac{3}{16}$
1856	$66\frac{1}{4}$	$4\frac{1}{2}$	$107\frac{1}{2}$	$4\frac{5}{8}$
1857	$66\frac{3}{4}$	$4\frac{1}{2}$	104	$4\frac{3}{4}$
1858	73	$4\frac{1}{8}$	$113\frac{1}{2}$	$4\frac{7}{16}$
1859	70	$4\frac{1}{4}$	110	$4\frac{1}{2}$
1860	$68\frac{1}{4}$	$4\frac{3}{8}$	$105\frac{1}{4}$	$4\frac{1}{16}$
1861	$67\frac{1}{4}$	$4\frac{7}{16}$	$98\frac{1}{8}$	$5\frac{1}{8}$
1862	$69\frac{1}{8}$	$4\frac{1}{4}$	97	$5\frac{3}{16}$
1863	$66\frac{1}{2}$	$4\frac{1}{8}$	$92\frac{1}{2}$	$5\frac{3}{8}$
1864	66	$4\frac{1}{2}$	89	$5\frac{5}{8}$
1865	68	$4\frac{3}{8}$	90	$5\frac{9}{16}$
1866	70	$4\frac{1}{4}$	$86\frac{1}{2}$	$5\frac{1}{4}$
1867	$68\frac{1}{2}$	$4\frac{3}{8}$	86	$5\frac{1}{4}$
1868	70	$4\frac{1}{4}$	$87\frac{1}{2}$	$5\frac{1}{16}$
1869	73	$4\frac{1}{8}$	86	$5\frac{1}{4}$
1870	54	$5\frac{9}{16}$	85	$5\frac{7}{8}$
1871	54	$5\frac{1}{16}$	91	$5\frac{5}{8}$
1872	$52\frac{1}{4}$	$5\frac{11}{16}$	95	$5\frac{1}{4}$
1873	$57\frac{1}{4}$	$5\frac{1}{4}$	97	$5\frac{3}{16}$
1874	$61\frac{1}{8}$	$4\frac{7}{8}$	102	$4\frac{7}{8}$
1875	66	$4\frac{1}{2}$	102	$4\frac{7}{8}$
1876	71	$4\frac{1}{4}$	79	$6\frac{5}{16}$

and more recently by a large creation of securities for railway purposes. Still the history is singularly on all-fours with that of Consols and the railway stocks selected for comparison, the same tendency to rise in value, that is to a diminished yield, in recent years being especially noticeable. The rise in French securities since the Franco-German war is in every way a remarkable fact.

Such have been the changes in the yield of Stock Exchange securities, and we have now to see whether the changes in the value of money, and in the yield of other securities, would be such as we should expect if what has happened in the securities mentioned fairly represents the general course of prices in them. To begin with money—it would be expedient to take into account the various descriptions of it dealt in, but to take only the most familiar test, that of the Bank of England rate of discount, there is obviously, we think, a history resembling the above history in securities. The average rates in each of the above periods we have selected for comparison have been — 1846-50, 3½ per cent ; 1851-55, 3*l*. 13*s*. per cent ; 1856-60, 4*l*. 6*s*. per cent; 1861-65, 4*l*. 18*s* per cent ; 1866-70, 3*l*. 11*s*. 6*d*. per cent ; 1870-75, 3*l*. 16*s*.

per cent; and 1876, 2⅝ per cent. Thus the rates were comparatively high just before 1850; comparatively low in the following decade especially in the first half of it; high in 1861-65; and since the latter date comparatively low, corresponding to the general tendency of securities to rise in the latter period. The movements do not exactly correspond, but there appears to be . sufficient nearness to show the working of the same general causes both in securities and money.

There have been similar changes in the rates for money employed in mortgages; a principal species of security not quoted on the Stock Exchange. There is a difficulty in quoting any general rates for English mortgages, although these are believed to have fallen greatly, but there happen to be means in Scotland for ascertaining general rates. In Edinburgh there are 'commissioners on the rate of interest,' who meet half yearly to fix the rate of interest on mortgages, and there is a similar body in Glasgow, whose proceedings supply us with interesting data on the subject. An Edinburgh friend has been good enough to send me the following memorandum :—

MEMORANDUM ON RATES OF INTEREST ON MORTGAGES IN SCOTLAND.

The Commissioners at Edinburgh are a body representing the Writers to the Signet, Solicitors before the Supreme Courts of Scotland, Chartered Accountants, and Ministers of Scotland Widows' Fund. Perhaps there may, from the constitution of this body be rather a leaning towards borrowers, as the interest of the Lawyers is to cultivate that connexion. The Insurance Companies were at one time parties in fixing the rate, but from some cause or other ceased to be so. They, however, do lend on the terms fixed by the Commissioners, though wherever there is any specialty in the nature of the loan (such, for instance, as loans for drainage, farm-buildings, &c. &c.), a somewhat higher rate is charged. It may also be mentioned that the large monied bodies, especially the Insurance Companies, now lend to Poor-Law Boards, School-Boards, Municipal Corporations, &c. &c. a good deal of money which formerly would have been invested in loans on land. These loans are negotiated at higher rates.

The Glasgow body came into existence in the year 1864, and the rates, since then—with the exception of a very short period—are the same as those fixed in Edinburgh.

The list subjoined may be considered as a correct statement of the rate at which money was lent on first-class Landed Security for the time specified :—

EDINBURGH COMMISSIONERS.

Interest received by the Widows' Fund of the Writers to the Signet, and other Incorporated Bodies, for sums invested on Landed Security.

From	To	Rate.	From	To	Rate.
Whits. 1817	Marts. 1822	5 per cent.	Whits. 1866	Marts. 1866	4½ per cent.
Marts. 1822	Whits. 1824	4½ ,,	Marts. 1866	Whits. 1867	5 ,,
Whits. 1824	Whits. 1826	4 ,,	Whits. 1867	Marts. 1867	4 ,,
Whits. 1826	Whits. 1828	5 ,,	Marts. 1867	Whits. 1868	4 ,,
Whits. 1828	Whits. 1829	4½ ,,	Whits. 1868	Marts. 1868	4 ,,
Whits. 1829	Marts. 1830	4 ,,	Marts. 1868	Whits. 1869	4 ,,
Marts. 1830	Lams. 1831	3½ ,,	Whits. 1869	Marts. 1869	4 ,,
Lams. 1831	Whits. 1834	4 ,,	Marts. 1869	Whits. 1870	4 ,,
Whits. 1834	Whits. 1837	3½ ,,	Whits. 1870	Marts. 1870	4 ,,
Whits. 1837	Marts. 1838	4 ,,	Marts. 1870	Whits. 1871	4 ,,
Marts. 1838	Marts. 1839	3½ ,,	Whits. 1871	Marts. 1871	4 ,,
Marts. 1839	Whits. 1843	4 ,,	Marts. 1871	Whits. 1872	4 ,,
Whits. 1843	Whits. 1846	3½ ,,	Whits. 1871	Marts. 1872	4 ,,
Whits. 1846	Marts. 1847	4 ,,	Marts. 1872	Whits. 1873	4 ,,
Marts. 1847	Whits. 1849	5 ,,	Whits. 1873	Marts. 1873	4 ,,
Whits. 1849	Marts. 1849	4½ ,,	Marts. 1873	Whits. 1874	4 ,,
Marts. 1849	Whits. 1850	4 ,,	Whits. 1874	Marts. 1874	4 ,,
Whits. 1850	Whits. 1854	3½ ,,	Marts. 1874	Whits. 1875	4 ,,
Whits. 1854	Marts. 1859	4 ,,	Whits. 1875	Marts. 1875	4 ,,
Marts. 1859	Whits. 1861	3½ ,,	Marts. 1875	Whits. 1877	4 ,,
Whits. 1861	Whits. 1866	4 ,,	Whits. 1877	Marts. 1877	4 ,,

GLASGOW BODY.

	Land.	Houses.
Marts. 1864 to Whits. 1867, both inclusive	4½ per cent.	5 per cent.
Marts. 1867 to Whits. 1877, both inclusive	4 ,,	4½ ,,

Analysing the above figures we find that while the rate on mortgages fixed by the Edinburgh Commissioners was as low as 3½ per cent from 1843 to 1846, it rose in the latter year to 4 per cent, and in 1847 to 5 per cent, which is the starting-point for our present comparison. This

rate was only maintained till 1849, when there
was a fall first to 4½ and then to 4 per cent, which
was succeeded in the following year by a further
decline to 3½ per cent, which continued for four
years. This was succeeded in 1854 by a 4 per
cent period, lasting five years; a 3½ per cent
period, beginning 1859, lasting two years; a 4 per
cent period beginning 1861, lasting five years; and
a short interval of 4½ and 5 per cent in 1866 and
1867; since which latter there has been a steady
rate of 4 per cent. The history has, therefore,
been that immediately after the beginning of the
free-trade period there was a comparatively high
rate, but this was followed between 1850 and 1866
by a long period of 3½ and 4 per cent rates to be
succeeded in turn by a short interval of dear
money, ending in another long period of low rates,
though not quite so low as in part of the period
between 1850 and 1866. The history of the
Glasgow body shows a corresponding movement
so far as the history extends, the last period of
high rates extending, however, from 1864 to 1867,
and being then followed by the low rates, which
corresponds still more closely to the course of rates
in the discount market in the period.

Money was cheap, and interest on securities

low, for a long period after 1850, but then there was a short period of dear money and cheap securities, arising no doubt from the great waste of capital prior to 1866, which has been succeeded by cheap money on the average, and high prices of securities, both those of the Stock Exchange and not of the Stock Exchange.

To conclude, the rates for money on mortgage have changed with the average rates in the short loan market, and in a direction conformable to that we should expect from a rise in securities. What has been the cause of this general fall recently in the rates obtainable by capitalists in the employment of their capital? of this general competition which has raised the price and diminished the yield obtainable from securities?

On the principles laid down in previous chapters, the answer must be that there has been one year with another no destruction of fixed capital lately, but on the contrary a steady increase of it, coupled with an increase of the surplus, whether of cash or consumable commodities, available to be lent or to be used for the purchase of securities. The only other cause assignable would be an increase of the quantity of money in proportion to transactions, but during the last ten years in

which the rise in securities has mainly taken place
the indications are that there has been no such
increase in the quantity of money in the world.
The annual supply of gold, which is the only money
we need here speak of, has rather fallen off in
recent years; there has simultaneously been an
increased demand for it for Germany; and the
price of commodities has not increased since 1868.
On the contrary, the average price of commodities
is believed to be now 10 per cent lower than in
1868, and to be almost at the level of 1861.*
The only cause of the low value of money and high
price, which means a low yield for investments,
must therefore be the pressure of a surplus for
investment. On the principles we have explained
the surplus need not be a very large one, for a
small quantity would have a great effect on price;
but that it has existed can hardly be doubted.
There is no other way of accounting for the phenomena of the last thirty years.

In point of fact, as far as cash is concerned,
there has been a manifest increase of this surplus.

* To prove this would require an elaborate statistical
examination of the facts, which would hardly be in place in
the present volume. I hope to communicate to the public
the results of such an examination in another form.

Leaving out Germany, which is a new competitor, the great commercial countries have all been accumulating larger and larger amounts of cash, the most remarkable accumulation, as is well known, being in the Bank of France. It may be said, of course, that this does not prove a surplus, because transactions may have increased proportionately, and the Banks really require the increased amount for their new liabilities. But the answer to this is, that at least in France, we know there has been no such increase of transactions, while in England the facilities for economising money are such that hardly any increase of transactions would count, so that the increase of the surplus cannot be explained in this way. On the other hand, it may be suggested that such an increase of money would raise prices as a mere increase of the quantity of money would, but to this the answer is that for such a purpose the increase seems to be altogether insignificant, while, as we have already suggested, there has been no general rise of prices but only a rise in securities, commodities having lately fallen in price.

An important conclusion may, we think, be drawn from this spectacle of a general fall in

money and rise in securities. This is—the un-
mistakable tendency there is for investment-
capital to increase without finding an adequate
outlet. The great rise since 1870 especially appears to show that there is hardly any limit to
the force of saving in the great communities of
modern times, and that the creation of good solid
securities cannot keep pace with it. People lay
past every year more than they can employ profitably in a reproductive manner, although every year
new reproductive employments are created. And
it does not seem unnatural that this should be so.
Pending the discovery of wants in society, for which
fixed capital is required, there is no way of convert-
ing circulating into fixed capital profitably, and
the means available for this conversion may also
be increased so rapidly that if a new way is found
the void is at once filled up. Consequently there
is almost always a surplus pressing for investment,
which appears never to be destroyed except in the
rare case of a great war like the Civil War in the
United States, or the perhaps rarer case of an
enormous destruction of capital on unproductive
works of a peaceful kind. But the reproductive
forces of modern communities are so great that
such voids are easily filled up. It is only six

years since the close of the Franco-German war, but the capital loss of the French people is already far more than covered, and the price of 3 per cent rentes, notwithstanding all the new creations, is not far short of what it was before the war.

The suggestion will be very natural that this view confirms the economic doctrine of the tendency of profits to a minimum. To avoid controversial matter I have endeavoured to state the facts so as merely to prove the points more directly connected with the object of the present essay. But the suggestion that the facts prove more than this, appears to be well founded. If there is a surplus pressing for investment, it seems obvious that it will not only help to diminish the rate obtainable by investors in purchasing old securities, it will also by competition help to lower the yield obtainable by all capital in securities. This is visibly so in the employment of capital on mortgages and short loans ; and although in monopoly business new capital cannot operate to reduce profits, it must operate as regards all other investments as it does on the short loan market. Many of these other investments are in reality permanent loans, the rates for which are lower than they would otherwise be in consequence of this competition—that being the meaning of the high price at which they are issued. In all cases besides, where the securities created are the shares of new companies, whose business is not a monopoly, their competition will clearly tend to keep down the rate of profit in the trade. The facts we have stated therefore, are really, as well as apparently, in conformity with the economic doctrine, and the explanation we have given would be unintelligible if that doctrine were untrue. In ordinary circumstances there is a tendency to a minimum in the profits of capital, and this tendency is only reversed either when there has been a large destruction of capital as in a great war, or when the need for new fixed capital of a productive kind is so great as to exceed the actual means of a community to supply it—cases of rare occurrence, while a great gap in capital may be filled up with surprising rapidity.

CHAPTER XII.

SUMMARY AND CONCLUSIONS.

IT may be convenient now to sum up the more important of the results which have been arrived at in the course of this inquiry. Having done so, we propose to add some practical reflections for the guidance of investors and dealers in securities.

The first conclusion we shall thus state is, that there is a natural limit in the amount of money to the aggregate price of all securities and commodities, and consequently a necessity is involved that a rise in commodities generally should produce a fall in securities, and *vice versâ*; in other words, that a rise or fall in any one article should tend to produce an opposite movement in all other articles. The operation of this limit is modified or obscured in actual life by changes in the state of credit, which enables the same amount of money at different times to sustain prices of securities and commodities together at different levels, and also by changes in the amount of commodities themselves ; but the natural limit must always exist, though we do not see it in operation.

2nd. An equal simultaneous nominal rise in the price of securities and commodities would mean a greater real rise in the securities, supposing the nominal income from the latter to remain unchanged, because the income would be less effective in purchasing than it was before. On the other hand, an equal simultaneous nominal fall might mean a greater real fall in the securities than in commodities, the income from the security becoming more effective with each fall in the commodities, so that it is a more valuable article than before. Consequently a fall in commodities and a rise in securities at the same time might be coincident with no real change in the effect of the same amount of money in procuring an income from investment at the time. A yield of four per cent, for instance, might be worth as much to an investor at one period as a yield of four and a half per cent at another.

3rd. The most important factor in the changes in the price of securities, as in the price of commodities—apart from changes in the income from the securities themselves—is the cyclical change in the state of credit which is now an established law of business. There is an ebb and flow in prices, and the general level is much higher at one time than another. At times of high price also, as part of the same general inflation, there is likely to be a large manufacture of fictitious securities, and a greater proportionate inflation of inferior securities as compared with the more solid article. It also follows that as securities and commodities rise and fall together in the cycle, the great nominal rise in securities at such times means a most excessive real rise. The nominal yield of investments is reduced, and the real value of the same nominal yield is less than it would be in times of low price for commodities. *Per contra*, in the times of low price, securities may not only exchange for a time at a lower nominal value than formerly, giving an increased nominal yield to the investor, but the same nominal yield would be more valuable than before, so that the real fall is greater than it appears, and tends immediately to produce a reaction in the price of the more solid securities.

4th. The manipulation of the stock markets,

through the processes of cornering and the like, though it may have a great effect on particular stocks, and at times may seem to have a considerable general effect when operators are fortunate enough to anticipate the working of real general causes, amounts by itself to very little. The movements resulting from any such manipulation are necessarily limited by the quantity of money; by the state of credit, and consequently the amount of illusion it is possible to create; by the calculation of the operators as to how they are to make a profit, profit being their object and not a mere desire to produce a great effect on prices; and by the 'conspiracy' of sensible men, who hold money or stocks, against any extreme which they know cannot be lasting, so that they enter into counter-operations long before the natural possibilities of the first unsound operation against which they work are exhausted. The incidents of the stock markets cannot, therefore, greatly modify or divert even for a time the working of the great natural laws.

Lastly, there is a *permanent* tendency to a rise in the price of securities through the want of suitable new outlets for accumulating surplus capital. This surplus may at no time be very great, because new wants grow with the increase of wealth, and fixed investments are always increasing; but a small surplus may have a great effect on price. The effect of this accumulating surplus is constantly operating through all the cyclical changes of credit, and probably helps to intensify the reaction in the price of solid securities immediately after a general fall, through the disposition to make new investments being less then than at other times. A great and protracted war, or a similar event, will counteract for a time this permanent tendency for a surplus to accumulate, by causing a large creation of new securities; but even an event like the Franco-German war has been found to be of very limited and temporary influence. During the last ten or fifteen years, it is possible to draw the conclusion from the actual facts of the rate of discount and the price of securities, both those quoted on the Stock Exchange and others, that the price of securities has risen, and the rate of yield obtainable on investments has declined.

The reflections which should occur to an investor upon these conclusions appear to be very obvious. It is plain, first of all, that there is always a danger of a partial loss of capital by any investment, apart from any question of its intrinsic unsoundness or the security of the income derived from it. Prices are constantly fluctuating from the state of the money market, the manipulations of the Stock Exchange, and a thousand causes; and although there are natural limits to the fluctuations, and they conform to general laws, which wise people may speculate upon, the great mass who have not the requisite data for speculating may lose by this incessant movement. By buying at a high price and being forced or induced for some reason to realise at a low price, their capital may dwindle away. It is no consolation to a particular investor that things right themselves in the aggregate; the difference of nominal capital is always most important, although the real yield of the reduced capital, *i.e.*, the amount of commodities which the income procures, may be as much or greater than it was when unreduced.

An investor, therefore, should in my opinion, no matter how solid the security may be or how trustworthy the income, always set aside a certain proportion of the income as sinking fund to guard against the danger of a loss of capital. There may be cases where it is of no consequence to do this, where capitals are large and are widely distributed among solid investments, so that the investor may trust to the permanent tendencies towards a rise in securities which we have described; but I should doubt whether the majority of investors are in this happy condition. For the sake of income they may consider it desirable to invest in securities not quite of the first class, or they may have only a small sum to invest in a few securities. As occasional realisations are unavoidable in the course of human affairs, there is consequently an unavoidable risk of loss of nominal capital, which must always be material to the mass of investors, and the only way to avoid it is to set aside a portion of the income for the express purpose of meeting this loss. Practically in fact, from an investor's point of view, the apparent yield of an investment should always be looked on as more than the real yield, because a deduction has to be made from it for this important purpose.

Considering how low the yield of good investments is, the advice given may seem hard; but saving money, and what is still more difficult keeping it, are matters lying outside the range of sentiment, and however desirable investors may think it to have an income secure against risk whether of principal or interest, it is impossible to alter the facts for their benefit. Hard as the recommendation is, it is accepted,

I believe, and acted upon by soundly conducted banks and other institutions which have reserves invested in the most solid and easily realisable securities, although in fact such institutions are no more likely to be forced to realise, are perhaps less likely to be so forced, than ordinary investors. What they do when they make a purchase of Consols, say, is to write off out of the income for a year or two a certain part of the price. One great joint-stock bank some time ago told its shareholders that its Consols stood in their books at 90, so that realising at any price above 90 would more than replace the capital invested to the bank. It is precisely this course which I recommend all investors to follow. They must not treat all the income they receive as income or profit, to spend or to save, but a portion must be treated as sinking fund to guard against the loss of original capital.

This leads me to suggest that in one particular the practice of the law courts and of trustees in dealing with trust moneys where the capital belongs to one *cestui que trust*, and the income to another, should be amended. A sharp line is now drawn between income and capital, and if a purchase of something yielding an income is made with the capital, the whole gross income is given to the owners of the income. If a change of investment is made, the loss, if any, falls upon the owner of the capital. But if there is a constant risk of a diminution of capital, the practice would seem to be erroneous. Out of the income a certain sum should always be set aside to replace the capital, if that capital is to remain intact. To apply a good and perfectly sound principle would no doubt be difficult for lawyers, but the point is one, considering the danger of loss there is, which ought not to be wholly ignored.

Another reflection which should be made by the investor is, that if he meddles only with the most solid securities and sets aside a moderate sinking fund, he runs little risk of losing his capital, especially as there is a permanent tendency to rise in price; but at the same time he should endeavour, if possible, not to invest when the pendulum has swung upwards, and to invest by preference when it has swung downwards. The higher the yield of a security and the lower its status, the more useful it will be to bear the maxim in mind. To a certain extent the endeavour to act on this rule will be a speculation on the part of an investor. He may confuse a rise in some particular security due to special and permanent causes, with a mere upward swing of the pendulum, which will come back again, and so may lose for ever the chance of a good investment. He may, on the contrary, confuse a fall from real causes which will also be permanent and increase with the mere downward swing of the pendulum. But there is no possibility of getting rid of some risk in the business of investing, and those concerned must make the best of it. It is still important to point out that there is an upward and downward swing, as of a pendulum, in the prices of securities, and that, other things being equal, an investor should choose his time. The times of inflation unfortunately mean that there is then a great deal of excited buying when people do not judge calmly, when they are led astray by illusions, when there is no visible sign of a possible or probable change in the state of credit. The ordinary investor must find it difficult to resist the influences of the moral atmosphere of such periods. All that can be done is to give the warning for those who care to profit by it. Probably few investors have suffered, however little they have been able to choose a cheap time to invest, if they have been careful to meddle only with the more solid securities, and have also been careful to set aside a sinking fund.

It must also be recognised that for ordinary investors a practical choice must often be made between buying at a high price or foregoing an income for the time. It does not always answer to wait, for there is a loss of interest in waiting. But I believe that almost always there would be little loss of interest by waiting at those times when the high prices are most dangerous. This is when the prices of commodities as well as of securities are at a high level. At such times, as a rule, the average rate of discount and the average allowances by bankers for money on deposit are temporarily high. Consequently the investor who waits can obtain for a time a fairly good rate for his money, with a practical certainty of keeping his capital intact, and if he can get about 3 to 4 per cent in this way, he has little occasion to hurry into permanent investments. It is seldom possible to obtain such rates for any length of time unless things have got to a high level, when a swing of the pendulum in the opposite direction may be looked for.

It is another most obvious reflection indeed that an investor must especially avoid touching

securities which have evidently been the subject
of Stock Exchange manipulation. He must not
buy after Stock Exchange speculators have bought;
and the greater and more persistent the rise, the
more careful he must be. The extreme brings strong
forces against it, and it is not infrequently a sign
of desperate speculation on the part of really insolvent operators. In the same way the investor
should be more careful than usual about selling,
when the Stock Exchange manipulators have sold.
If there has been an extreme rig downwards, the
probability, at least as regards securities of any
solidity, is that the causes of the fall are fully dis-
counted. This rule must not, however, be understood to mean that the investor is in no case to
buy or sell in the cases mentioned. The great
movement which has taken place may possibly be
deserving of his attention. Especially in the case
of an organized attack upon a particular security,
before a general depression has come, it frequently
happens that the Stock Exchange speculator is
unable to discount fully, owing to the danger of
the operation, the real causes of depreciation at
work. The higher the yield of interest on any
such attacked security, the more disposed should
an investor be to accept the warning given by the

Stock Exchange operator. But the warning or hints are likely to be most useful, if at all, in stocks with which ordinary investors should have little to do. In the more solid stocks it remains the rule of prudence not to buy or sell after the Stock Exchange operators, but to hold back, or even to act in an opposite sense to these operators.

It is not perhaps, strictly speaking, a deduction from anything laid down or demonstrated in the present book, but it may be permissible for the writer nevertheless to add an opinion he has formed as to what should be the conduct of investors in another particular. This opinion is, that investors should form judgments for themselves in buying and selling, based on a careful examination of the facts which determine the value of the securities, and should *not* be guided by the opinions of bankers, brokers, solicitors, or other friends whom they may consult in the matter. Their knowledge of the nature of securities may be limited, and the rule may apparently shut them out altogether from securities which yield more than the lowest rate of interest ; but the reasons for it seem to me absolutely conclusive. It is quite plain that advice in such matters can only be given and received at particular moments, whereas to avoid loss constant attention must be paid to the subject. A friend, for instance, may think that a particular joint-stock company is not only admirably managed at the time his opinion is asked for, but that it is so conditioned that a change to bad management is hardly conceivable. The directorate may be large and wealthy, and composed of men who give ample time to the management of a business in which they are deeply interested. The friend accordingly advises the would-be investor who consults him that shares in such a company, in all human probability, would be a good investment. But a year or two passes. The directorate does in fact change, through a slight infusion of new blood; accidents happen; the wealthy proprietors and directors sell their shares; what seemed a good investment becomes a very bad one. Probably the keen-judging adviser is not himself hurt by this, because he knows the real nature of such securities, and being constantly mixed up in business with them has accepted a timely warning. But the investor whom he advised momentarily knows nothing and hears nothing, and is involved in the adversity which his original adviser escapes. In the nature of things it is not to be expected that the adviser would remember gratuitous opinions and advice he had given years before; and not being consulted again at the right moment, his newer knowledge, without any fault of his, is of no value to the man whom he advised. It is the same with state loans, preference shares, debentures, everything in the nature of a security. In this changing world no security continues for a long period in precisely the same conditions, and therefore no occasional advice by friends can be of much value to investors. This would be the case if the advice were always well considered, and given by people who fully realised the situation of those inquiring. But the readiest to advise are most frequently the sanguine and buoyant, who have no fear for themselves and others, who take great risks themselves, and think that others may do the same. There is also no small danger of corrupt or biassed advice, though I am here arguing mainly on the supposition that the experts, or supposed experts, whom investors consult are really trustworthy in intention. In any case gratuitous advice would be little trusted by wise men in any other important affair; and all I maintain is, that it is not to be trusted, but rather to be specially distrusted, in securities. And not taking advice, there is nothing of course for investors but·to follow their own judgment, and keep to what they understand. Be it bonds, or mortgages, or consols, or the debentures and preference shares of joint-stock companies, let them keep to what they know something about, and take all the risks themselves. There is no outside judgment which can really be made available for them.

The difficulty of investors would not perhaps be so great if they could avail themselves of the same good outside help without any change—if they had an acute friend always at their elbow to advise them. It appears to me a great stretch of friendship to try the good-nature of a friend to the extent that the hypothesis supposes—to expect him to keep in mind all your investments as well as his own, and give you all the benefit of his skill and experience—to think for you as well as himself, when he may be really puzzled about his own line of action. Still, this is the only condition upon which it will be safe to rely on outside help; you must have one continuous adviser with whom, if necessary, you periodically consult. In fact, however, investors who lean on outsiders will probably run from one to another;

and although any one might have been a safe
guide, single mistakes being rectified by general
good sense, yet the multiplicity of advisers will
be ruin. Now one, now another opinion, will be
followed, and sometimes, out of sheer distraction,
a wrong course, which was not really advised by
any one consulted, will be taken. Investors have
thus no means of escaping from the necessity of
judging for themselves.

Some readers may perhaps think that what I
have written is such obvious common sense that
there was no occasion to write it. But those who,
like myself, have often been asked to give opinions,
will know best how utterly devoid of common
sense the average investor is on this subject.
Scores and hundreds of times I have been asked
questions whether such and such a security, paying six or seven per cent, or perhaps even a higher
rate of interest, was 'safe'—a question which
could not be answered without a knowledge of
the affairs of the applicant you could not always
possess, and without a long examination of the
applicant as to what he meant by safety, and an
exposition to him of the most disagreeable doctrine, that no security could be absolutely safe.
But in many cases, while avoiding giving opinions

as much as possible, I have often had reason to know that the applicants were ready to construe the slightest glimpse of an opinion, the slightest hint that 'good people' were buying or selling the security in question, into an opinion that they might go and do likewise, the conviction on their part being invincible that prudence prevented one from giving direct advice, but that they had got to the bottom of one's mind for all that. People believe that they are entitled to a high rate of interest, and they are so infatuated as to think any good opinion, however slight, will be an excuse for their taking up an investment paying a high rate. When the ruin comes they are loud in bewailing their luck, or censuring the judgment they suppose they have followed; they do not recognise that their own greed or folly had blinded them to the actual facts of the world, and that they had merely been beaten in the game of chess, having made an unsound move, by the inexorable chess-player. In my semi-public capacity as a City editor I have come across the most curious illustrations of the strength and persistency of the belief that investors have a right to high interest, and that they are to be taken care of. More than once I

M

have received protests against publishing news affecting a particular security, because it depressed the price. The news in one case I have in my mind was of the utmost value, as foreshadowing a collapse in the security itself, although it could only be published at the time for what it was worth; and for the benefit of the whole public interested, *i.e.*, the possible investors as well as the present holders. But I was informed that my duty as City editor was, not to give news or information, but to keep stocks at their proper prices—that I was to be the providence of investors, and give them opinions to go by, and *not* give them data on which to found judgments of their own. Such letters, and other facts which have come to my knowledge, have given me a deep conviction of the utter unreasonableness of many of the public about securities, and of the necessity of more education on the subject. There can be no doubt that the whole fabric of bubble companies and bubble loans in prosperous times has its foundation in this diffused insanity of the public on a matter of vital interest. Advertisements and prospectuses are circulated, because the public will believe anything, and City editors and other experts, or supposed experts, are followed in their slightest hints of opinion, however carefully they may protest against being supposed to give an opinion, however little the public may sometimes know of their qualifications to have an opinion in a given case, and however impossible it may be for any man to give opinions which could be safely used by a mixed multitude, whose conditions and objects in a particular investment cannot but vary indefinitely. There is no remedy but to preach incessantly the necessity which is laid upon investors to judge for themselves, in the hope that here and there some one or two may be the better for the preaching.

LONDON:
Printed by JOHN STRANGEWAYS, Castle St. Leicester Sq.

Lightning Source UK Ltd.
Milton Keynes UK
UKHW031345281019
352454UK00010B/2613/P